Wedding Bouquets and Flowers

JILL WOODALL

Wedding Bouquets and Flowers

JILL WOODALL

THE CROWOOD PRESS

First published in 2017 by
The Crowood Press Ltd
Ramsbury, Marlborough
Wiltshire SN8 2HR

www.crowood.com

British Library Cataloguing-in-Publication Data
A catalogue record for this book is available from the British Library.

ISBN 978 1 78500 270 0

Typeset by Sharon Dainton
Printed and bound in India by Replika Press Pvt Ltd

Contents

Preface

My introduction to the world of flowers began, as it does for so many of us, when I was a child. I remember meadows swaying with tall grasses, moon daises nodding their heads, purple clover underfoot and bright red poppies dotted in random swaths of colour. Hedgerows that were not only handy hiding places, but also gave us hawthorn berries and blackberries to forage. Dark, quiet, and mysterious woodlands where dappled rays of the sun shone down on carpets of spring bluebells, with pungent wild garlic filling the air. Bright green moss clinging in crevices on old stone walls, growing in wet and soggy clumps on the woodland floor and creeping over dead tree stumps only to be interrupted by unfurling fronds of fern.

Lime green catkins that appeared like velvet to the naked eye showered plumes of pollen when touched, and who could resist picking twigs of soft, silky, white pussy willow. In fields where mushroom fairy rings could be chanced upon we would dance around to make a wish. Mature trees with their large canopy of branches made shelters from the sun where one would sit and while away the time, or climb to the top for that ultimate lookout post. In the autumn, cobnuts, brown shiny conkers and chestnuts with green prickly husks were plentiful. And of course, every little girl knew how to make daisy chains into circlets, necklaces and bracelets. A carefully picked posy was all it took to engage my passion for flowers. But the greatest pleasure for me was to see the delight on my mother's face when she was presented with this wild bunch. I still feel the same pleasure and delight today when presenting brides with their freshly made wedding bouquets.
The flowers I gave my mother that day took pride of place on the kitchen windowsill in a mix-and-match of old jam jars and milk bottles. After a few days the lifeless brown twigs with large sticky buds burst into life and developed into bright green leaves. It was magical, and turned my inquisitive mind to all the things that nature could show me.

Today when learning floral art, students are encouraged to observe nature in all its forms (the seeing eye). This helps to identify growth, texture, form, colour, space and harmony, all of which are key to understanding and practising floral art, which seeks to bring order out of chaos. I hope this book will be a foundation on which to build your confidence and inspire you to produce your own creative and unique floral art.

Teaching at my flower school (www.bristolflowerschool.co.uk) and pleasing others is a reward in itself, so go on, make a bride happy!

LEFT: English bluebell wood.

Chapter 1

The History of Wedding Floristry

Plant material has been used for decoration and symbolism since early civilization, and consciously or unconsciously we still partake in rites and rituals long associated with wedding flowers today. How wonderful it is that in the twenty-first century we continue on with traditions practised thousands of years ago.

Although modern brides may have little understanding of the original importance of flowers at weddings, they certainly would not think of walking down the aisle without carrying flowers in some shape or form. Why is this? Let's start to answer that question by taking a look at the history of wedding flowers and how that usage has evolved over time.

The Egyptian Era: c. 3000–332BC

The Egyptians left a wealth of information recorded in their hieroglyphs and paintings, and preserved in their tombs. They were agricultural people living in peace on the banks of the River Nile, enabling them to cultivate many plants and flowers, which were sometimes used as religious offerings, including to the fertility gods. Osiris was seen as the mother god of all growing things and was honoured with flowers by those hoping for a happy, long life. Women during this period were seen wearing chaplets and headbands consisting of blue cornflower, white mayweed and pink flowers; collars of papyrus, olive, pomegranate, and willow leaves folded as clasps to hold water-lily petals; and holding gorgeous bouquets of papyrus, lotus and poppy. There is no evidence of these flowers being worn by brides and grooms, but as they were used for special ceremonies this may have included weddings. The blue water lily, whose perfume was said to be a sexual stimulus, was used to make wax cones. The cones could be seen attached to headbands worn by women. In the heat, the cones would gradually melt and cover their wearers' bodies with perfume. Roots of the mandrake were also dug up and used to make love potions.

The Greek and Roman Eras: 600–146BC and AD28–325

The Greek and Roman periods were very similar in climate and flora. Greeks and Romans recorded many details about plants and flowers and featured them in mosaics, carvings on vases, and wall paintings, as seen in The Aldobrandini Wedding held in the Vatican Library in Rome. Greeks and Romans appreciated beauty in all its forms and used plant material to honour their gods, especially Flora, the goddess of flowers and spring, and Juno, the goddess of marriage. It is during this period that we see the first

The Greco-Roman God Hymen with nuptial crown.

LEFT: Brides throughout history have worn chaplets of flowers.

9

Garland makers in the Market Place.

evidence of flowers being crafted specifically for weddings.

Marriage ceremonies in these times were carried out in the home, not in a temple. The bride dressed in a long white tunic with a girdle tied round her waist in a double knot, called the knot of Hercules. A transparent flame-coloured veil covered her face and her head was crowned with a garland of myrtle and orange blossom. Saffron-coloured sandals were worn and the outfit was finished with a yellow cloak. The bride would have had bridesmaids to assist her and they all, along with the guests and the groom, wore flower crowns. Interestingly, the person who carried the bride over the threshold of her new home would have been the best man, not the bridegroom. The bridal procession to the groom's house was led by a young boy carrying a 'Ceres' torch to light the way, and the doors of the groom's house and the bridal bed were garlanded with roses and myrtle. Myrtle was also placed in large pedestal vases for wedding preparations, and as an offering to Venus.

A popular florist, famous for making wreaths and garlands, and written about during 380BC, was Glycera of Sicyon.

Such wreaths were not only worn on the head, but as garlands hung around the neck or over one shoulder and across the body. Roman chaplet 'crowns' were also made with violets, saffron and red roses, bright mixed colours, and were tied at the back of the head with ribbons hanging down the wearer's back. In Athens, crowns were sold in what was called a 'myrtle market' even long after this plant was toppled from popularity by other flowers.

In Roman times, Ceres was the goddess of agriculture, and crops and flowers were given as offerings for her protection by women transitioning from girlhood (girls could marry from the age of twelve) to womanhood, from unmarried to married. Poppies were also associated with Ceres for the large amount of seeds they produced; offerings to Ceres would hopefully ensure a bride's fertility. Another important deity for weddings at this time was the god Hymenaeus. Lyrics were sung to him on the bridal procession to the groom's house.

On festival and ceremonial occasions flowers and petals were strewn on floors, tables and beds. The revolving ceiling in Emperor Nero's Golden House opened up to shower his guests with flowers and a cloud of rose petals, suffocating some guests under the weight.

The Italian Renaissance: 1400–1600

Prosperity during this time not only allowed easier travel, urban development and trading further afield, but an increase in the arts. The middle classes could now afford paintings to show off their wealth, and we can see in these paintings evidence of the dresses and flowers brides were wearing. Prior to this, paintings were only seen in churches to the glorification of God.

The first evidence of lilies being used

as a symbol of purity is seen alongside the Virgin Mary in Hugo van der Goes' altarpiece painting. Ever since, the white Madonna lily has symbolized virginity. Florentine ladies revived the Greek and Roman tradition of wearing garlands of flowers on their heads. These were later made by goldsmiths with precious stones and gold, very much like the tiaras worn by brides today.

The Late Middle Ages: c. 1301–1500

Saracen brides wore crowns of orange blossom, a tradition brought to Europe by the Crusaders. Saxon brides and grooms both wore garlands of flowers including myrtle, rosemary and cornflowers, which were sometimes kept in the church for such occasions.

The Tudor Period: 1488–1603

Renaissance arts and crafts spread to England in this time of relative peace. Botanists' newly discovered plants and flowers were brought to England and copied, as seen in many embroideries and tapestries with floral motifs. The Tudor rose, with red petals on the outside and white in the middle, became symbolic of the Tudor period upon the marriage of Henry Tudor, a Lancastrian (the red rose), to Elizabeth of York (the white rose). Anne of Cleves, on the other hand, is recorded to have had a sprig of myrtle in her wedding bouquet when she married Henry Tudor. Paintings also show us gilded rosemary worn on the hats and sleeves of men. In *A Fete at Bermondsey*, the 1569–70 painting by Joris Hoefnagel, a bridal cup being carried to the ceremony is constructed of rosemary, ribbons (bridal laces) and flowers. The latter are not so easy to identify but are thought to be either roses or pinks.

In homes during this period we see a

Tudor tussie-mussie.

strewing of plant material on tables, maybe herbs and petals, and also trees or branches of foliage lined around the inside walls of the building. Garlands of finely gilded wheat are recorded to have been used at weddings but there is no mention of how this gilding was carried out. Also seen in many paintings were 'tussie-mussies' or nosegays, simple, hand-tied bunches of sweetly perfumed flowers, usually roses, pinks, violets, primroses, cornflowers, lavender and honeysuckle, carried to ward off disease, plague and the smell of unwashed bodies. 'A nosegay bound with ribbons in his hat, bride laces, sir, and his hat all green' is mentioned in a poem by H. Porter in 1599. Pomanders (oranges stuck all over with cloves and tied with ribbons, carried over the wrist, in the hand or hanging from the waist) were also popular for their sweet smell.

The Georgian Period 1714–1830

This was known as the 'age of elegance'. Prosperity for the Georgians brought in artists and craftsmen of all kinds. Wood furniture became more refined and decorative with the import of mahogany, walnut, inlays of satinwood and painted borders, some of which now included flowers. Silk materials were heavily woven with flowers and used for curtains, drapes, furniture and clothes. Flowers were worn on high piled-up

hairstyles, attached to dresses, bosoms or shoulders, and mixed flowers were carried in baskets and as posies. Overall the style was open and elegant with no added foliage, soft subtle pastels, and peach, apricot, rose pink, cream, blue, mauve and grey-green colours were preferred.

With the growing production of porcelain and ceramics came many styles of vase; sometimes vases in pairs would be placed on either end of white marble mantelpieces, their flowers placed in a mass, loose style arrangement. Roses are still very much in evidence at this time, along with peonies, lilac, trailing vines of honeysuckle and graceful catkins. A famous wood carver of the time, Grinling Gibbons, incorporated long catkin flowers in many of his designs, most notably on fireplaces.
The overall style of the early Georgian period was Baroque, showing us glowing rich colours, followed by the French Rococo influence and later by the Regency period when a delicate, elegant, restrained period of flower-arranging appeared.

The Rococo Period: 1715–1774

Before the French Revolution the aristocracy was notoriously extravagant: garlands of flowers were worn across the body, chaplets adorned heads and nosegays were carried with pretty ribbons. Flowers on dining tables were elaborate, excessive and included branches of trees. The Empress Josephine (1763–1814) collected all known species of rose in her garden at Château de Malmaison, where French nurserymen carried out hybridizing on a large scale.

The Victorian Era: 1830–1901

The Industrial Revolution brought with it

great wealth. Houses were stuffed full of every trinket and item of furniture that money could buy. There was a trend for hothouses to grow and show off the many new plants brought in by botanists and garden designers. As well as looking to paintings for evidence of this, we now have magazines, books and photography.

Harsh, contrasting coloured flowers in tight circles of concentric rows with lace edging were the fashion for wedding posies in the early Victorian period. The later period favoured a more open shower bouquet, sometimes seen with a good backing of lace. Garlands of fresh or wax orange-blossom flowers were worn on dresses, and in the hair of brides who could afford them. Ivy, ferns, including asparagus and maidenhair, smilax, myrtle, grey leaves and grasses were popular for decorating the home. Posies and bouquets had holders made from gold and silver filigree set with jewels with mother-of-pearl handles; other materials used were enamel, porcelain and crystal. These holders were worn attached to the dress with a pin on a chain.

Up to this period only the affluent could afford white wedding dresses; the majority were just a bride's best dress, usually brown or violet, which could be worn again. Princess Alice was the first English bride to be photographed at her wedding on 1 July 1862, wearing a white crinoline dress with garlands of myrtle. She had orange blossom in her hair and stitched to the hem of her dress. A year later, the second of Queen Victoria's daughters was photographed at her wedding and the pictures were flashed around the world. Now more people could see the latest fashion and try to copy it.

The 'language of flowers' was a popular way to send and receive messages between lovers in this era. Specific blooms were chosen to convey

Victorian wedding.

sentiments that Victorian protocol restricted. In this way, messages could be kept a secret from strict parents.

Art Nouveau and the Edwardian Period: 1890–1914

The lavish spending of the wealthy eventually led to the uprising of the working classes, the suffragette movement and trade unions. Women were seeking more recognition, and finally gained the right to vote in 1928. The clutter of the Victorian period was gradually being discarded, replaced with simpler lines seen in the sinuous stylistic flowers on furniture, architecture and dresses. This new art style (Art Nouveau) swept Europe and can be seen at some metro station entrances in Paris, in buildings in Spain and houses in England, at Hill House in Helensburgh in the Arts and Crafts style, and at the tea rooms in Charles Rennie Mackintosh's School of Art in Scotland. Butterfly and dragonfly motifs were popular, as were peacock feathers. Wedding dresses became straighter, made from softer chiffon and lace materials. Large flowing shower bouquets cascading down to the hem of the wedding dress were assembled with fern, smilax, roses, carnations and chrysanths. Bridesmaids carried similar bouquets to the bride and wore large decorated hats.

The Inter-War Period: 1920s–1939

The period following the First World War marked the beginning of the modern age. Corsets and long dresses made way for short skirts and dresses, and long, teased-up hair became bobbed and sleek. Flowers were used in a simple, naturalistic way. 'Every flower should be put in the way it grows,' advised Mrs Beeton. Constance Spry made this style of arranging flowers into an art form in the 1930s. Flowers floating in a shallow bowl were popular.

Although the wedding dress became shorter in length, brides still carried either a large flowing bouquet of fern, smilax, roses, chrysanthemums and orchids trailing down to the floor or the modern girl opted for the simpler sheaf of white arum lilies tied with ribbon on

Edwardian wedding.

1920: short skirts and lilies over the arm.

1920–1930: Dutch bonnets and flower-filled baskets for bridesmaids.

bare stems carried over the arm. Buttonhole or corsage flowers were limited to three at the most (usually one), with fern. Orchids were considered the most sophisticated choice. In 1929, the legal age for a girl to marry was changed from twelve years old to eighteen (or sixteen with parental consent) and to sixteen in Scotland.

Wartime and Early Post-War England: 1939–1950s

During this time, austerity and clothes rationing called for brides to find alternative fabrics for wedding dresses. Valuable silk parachute material was seized upon and refashioned into bridal dresses and underwear. As land was

needed for growing vegetables it was illegal for farmers to sow more than 10 per cent of a field with flowers. This small amount was to enable them to

1940: the war years – suits with corsages and a jaunty hat.

carry stock for cultivation after the war. Houses with back gardens were now turned into vegetable patches, leaving only the small front garden for flowers. With the selection of flowers diminished, it meant brides during and just after the war years had to make do with a corsage pinned to the lapel of a suit. A 'bible spray' of flowers attached to a wide ribbon used as a bookmark was also popular. The longer end of the ribbon was threaded through the book, usually marking the 'Solemnization of Matrimony' pages! As many women served in the war, weddings with both bride and groom in uniform became quite normal, and because of rationing, civilian brides tended to wear a neat, practical suit and a jaunty little hat with a scrap of veiling just covering the face. For the bride who could save enough of her clothes coupons to afford a traditional white wedding, the bouquets consisted of large, trailing ferns, roses, carnations and sometimes orchids. Orchids were grown in hothouses, not needing land for their cultivation, and were used for Princess Elizabeth's wedding bouquet to Prince Philip in

1940–1950: traditional dress, if war coupons were traded in for wedding material.

1960: the florist's nickname for a headdress with a central flower was a 'miner's lamp'.

1947.

The early fifties saw a return of the long wedding dress and shower bouquet, still with ferns in the Edwardian manner, though the huge size was not revived and more thought was given to the proportions of the bouquet to the dress and veil. By the mid-fifties short dresses also came into fashion and bouquets became much smaller and daintier with freesias, tulips, lily-of-the-valley and orchids.

Wartime bombing had caused the destruction of thousands of houses, leaving many people homeless and displaced. By the end of the fifties, large housing estates were being built, the utilitarian furniture of the war years was gradually being replaced, television was taking hold and a new modern age was emerging.

The Sixties: 1960–1969

All thoughts of the war years were now firmly set aside with a new generation of independent 'baby boomers'. Full

employment meant an income that could be spent on luxury goods and new off-the-peg youth fashions. The end of the sixties saw furnished homes with sleek plastic furniture, bright orange upholstery and shag pile carpets. Brides also broke away from anything from the past and gained fiercely fought independence from their parents. The early sixties brides wore ballerina-length wedding dresses tailored neatly at the waist, influenced by American movie stars and the introduction of rock and roll via the GIs in the war years. Bouquets became very neat, and were often in the shape of a teardrop. Fern was still the favoured foliage and was used along with roses, freesias and carnations in cream and white with pastels picking up the colours of the bridesmaids' dresses (often lemon, tangerine and apricot). Short bouffant veils were held in place with a large real or silk flower on the top of the head, which became known in the trade as the

Miniskirts, big hats, and the 'little girl' look.

'miner's lamp'! From the mid-1960s, stephanotis and pipped hyacinths had gained popularity as inclusions in wired headdresses and bouquets. In the later sixties miniskirts and hotpants took the place of wedding dresses with brides carrying small, simple posies, and wearing floppy hats or lacy headscarves, sporting the 'little girl' look, influenced by the models and pop stars of the time. Buttonholes for the men were carnations and fern, often seen with silver-foil-wrapped stems.

The Seventies: 1970–1979

Hippy trends became popular during this period: 'flower power', free love, loose flowers and garlands in the hair, brides carrying a single flower or a few stems of simple blooms. Wedding dresses with yokes and high necklines became fashionable, with long gathered sleeves similar in style to the Edwardian and Victorian era. Bridesmaids looked like old-fashioned country girls in Laura Ashley cotton frocks. Bouquets harked back to the Victorian posy of mixed flowers or a simple bunch of white daisies or marguerites. Small bridesmaids carried flower balls on long ribbons, made with roses, daisies or chrysanthemums. Flared trousers, waistcoats and shirts with oversized collars were now the fashion for the groom's outfit. Disco dancing now took the place of the bride and bridegroom's first waltz. In wider society, the end of the seventies introduced credit cards, financing home appliances, houses and cars.

The Eighties: 1980–1989

Big sleeves, big hair and shoulder pads were the fashion staples of the Dynasty-inspired era of the 1980s. Lady Diana Spencer's wedding to Prince Charles in 1981 was to guide wedding fashion for the next ten years. The new princess wore a full, billowing, silk dress, with puffed-up sleeves finished with lace and a long, sweeping train. Her shower bouquet trailed forty-two inches long and took five florists four hours each to make. Two identical bouquets were made, one for the ceremony and one for the photos. The bouquets contained orchids, gardenias, lily-of-the-valley, yellow 'Mountbatten' roses, stephanotis, myrtle taken from Osborne House and ivy. Their significant size sparked a trend for large bouquets amongst brides. These did not always include the most expensive blooms, but were as large as could be managed with alternative flowers. Bouquets of this size took skilful wiring so were priced accordingly at £250–£350. This made a dramatic change from the smaller posies or single flowers of the seventies.

Foam posy holders now overtook wired designs, as the ease of their construction and the improved lifespan they gave some flowers meant that hours of wiring work were no longer essential. Florists were now at their busiest, creating large bouquets, and smaller, matching bouquets for the bridesmaids, circlet headdresses, hoops, baskets and buttonholes for all the guests. There were not only churches to decorate but also separate reception venues. Peach or soft pink roses, carnations, gypsophila and freesias were the flowers of the day, matching the shiny synthetic material of bridesmaids' dresses, made all too frilly with gathered puffy sleeves, gathered waistbands with a bow at the back and stiff petticoats. Table decorations, brides' and bridesmaids' bouquets, headdresses and buttonholes all included sprigs of gypsophila. Everything had the pretty princess 'fairy tale' look. 'Immortals' or dried flowers also made a comeback, both for young bridesmaids' baskets and to decorate the home. The recession or economic downturn affected savings and loans, and created a crisis at the end of the 1980s which saw the start of recycled furniture given a wash of paint and prettied up, now known as the 'shabby chic' style.

The Nineties: 1990–1999

By the mid-nineties, peach bridesmaids' dresses had given way to deep burgundy, crimson and midnight blue cotton dresses toned with gold. Circlet headdresses and Alice bands looked heavier with berries, roses and dark green ivy. 'Star Gazer' lilies were introduced and became the flower of the day. With a strong perfume and deep burgundy pink centres, the lilies had become firm favourites for brides' shower bouquets along with hypericum berries that had gradually taken over from gypsophila. Candles and ivy in terracotta pots were popular for table

Stargazer lilies were now the fashion.

decorations with plenty of butter muslin swags for the top table.

The Marriage Act of 1994 granted venues a license to conduct marriage ceremonies in buildings other than places of worship. Themed weddings started to evolve. This challenged florists to design extremely varied and sometimes wacky bouquets. Between Dracula dress codes and period drama costumes, conventional bridesmaids' dresses became somewhat redundant. When it came to flowers, orange calla lilies were interspersed with orange roses; hips and berries teamed with gold tiaras also defined this period, matching the champagne, oyster and doe skin shades of silk dupion bridal dresses. The new white Casablanca lilies took over from Star Gazers, and were teamed with white Singapore orchids to create huge shower bouquets, which became a clear favourite. Lilies were also used in tall, slim, glass vases on tables at the wedding venue, but on a hot day their strong perfume overpowered many a wedding reception room to a point of suffocation. In September 1997, on the death of Princess Diana, so many white lilies were diverted to London that some florists could not fulfil their wedding orders and some even cancelled their wedding orders altogether.

At the beginning of the nineties, the hand-tied 'just picked' bouquet was introduced but didn't gain popularity until the middle of the decade. Using simple daisy chrysanths with just a few other choice flowers slotted in, and tied with ribbons and bows, these were quick and easy to make, and were very economical for the bride but a loss of revenue for the florist. At a fraction of the price of a shower bouquet, by the end of the nineties many brides opted for this cheaper alternative, if not for themselves then certainly for the bridesmaids.

The Marriage Act of 1994 not only made it legal for civil ceremonies to take place in various licensed venues, it also sanctioned weddings on Sundays, meaning florists were now working a seven-day week.

The Millennium Begins: 2000–2007

The new millennium saw houses being stripped of many original features and wallpaper and being given a clean makeover of magnolia paint, otherwise known as the 'blank canvas look'. Silver had taken over from gold, and softer lavenders and mint greens became bridesmaids' colours. Lisianthus, which resembles the rose and was introduced in the nineties, became a valid newcomer for its variety of colours, which include purple, lavender and green blooms. The long, slender, clean lines of the calla lily took the place of the large Casablanca lilies and the moth orchid replaced the Singapore orchid. Wedding dresses favoured slim lines, with no fuss, lace or flounces. Hand-tied bouquets became compact, neat and tidy, often just white roses packed tightly together and embedded with diamond pins, surrounded with collars of aspidistra or fatsia leaves. Foliage and fussy table posies gave way to fresh, clean glass vases placed on mirrors surrounded by tea lights. Fish bowls, usually holding just a few arum lilies curled around inside or floating gerberas, made up the centrepieces on tables. 'Sprinkles' scattered around each and every plate were now all the fashion. Aluminium and bullion wires, diamonds and beads used to accessorize bouquets added distinction with twinkly jewel-like qualities. Decorative wire or satin ribbon stuck with pearl-headed pins or shiny buckles now adorned the stems of the hand-tied bouquet. Bouquets made entirely of wire and beads with glued-on orchids and twisting calla lilies fitted well with the new century, and flower circlets made way for tiaras.

The Recession: 2008–2016

In 2008, the collapse of the housing market saw 'austerity' measures coming into force and interest in nostalgia and 'tracing one's ancestors' growing. Catherine Middleton's marriage to Prince William in 2011 was not ostentatious, and the church 'tree decorations' were recycled after the wedding, but it was nonetheless a welcome and uplifting sight. Although Catherine's wedding dress has not been copied in full, the lace of the bodice has been incorporated into much that is associated with weddings today. Her dainty teardrop bouquet has also not been copied, partly due to its cost and the personal interpretation of the flowers it contained: White Sweet William for Prince William, white hyacinths and lily-of-the-valley for perfume. The lily-of-the-valley was influenced by Catherine's mother Carole Middleton's bouquet in 1981, and was used in Catherine's bridesmaid's bouquets and in their hair. A spring of myrtle taken from Queen Victoria's bouquet was planted at Osborne House and the bush is now the source of myrtle picked and included in every royal bride's bouquet today.

Brides are now opting for lace on the bodices of their dresses or a full-length, softer, slim-line lace dress. Hand-tied bouquets are now looser in style, with brides opting for peonies, English country roses, hydrangea and mixed flowers in peach, green and pink, tied with lace or satin ribbon bows. Birdcages, hurricane lamps and candles encircled with flowers are often used for table decorations. The 'vintage look' may also be teamed with glamorous silver candelabras and lace runners on tables and 'antimacassars' or cloth covers on chairs. Recycled furniture is whitewashed and glammed up.

Outside of the wedding sphere, homes have been made more comfortable and colour is returning to interior decorating. Remembering the end of the Second World War, 2015 saw a revival of the concept of 'make do and mend', with fragments of lace juxtaposed with hessian potato sacking, and string, brown paper, luggage tags, apple crates, recycled jam jars and bunting everywhere. Milk churns are used as containers for English country flowers, and meadow boxes and wooden ladders are used to stack pretty knick-knacks. Bouquets have taken on the 'rustic' look with meadow-picked country flowers. 'Woodland' wedding-themed venues are decorated using slices of natural wood as bases for jars and bottles filled with simple flowers. Larger arrangements favour the loose, open and flowing 'Constance Spry' style of the 1940s and 1950s, following in line with the vintage look.

Summary

Changes in styles of wedding flowers are a direct result of our economic, religious and social lives. The earliest years of marriage rites and rituals carried out by brides were intended to honour gods for a good and fruitful marriage by offering wheat for fertility, white lilies to symbolize purity and perfumed flowers and sweet-smelling herbs to mask body odour. Much of this is now outdated with the advent of IVF, the invention of deodorant, the waning of Christianity and other social changes.

Migration and an evolving religious landscape, among other things, have contributed to a society that sees fewer traditional English church weddings. Brides' lives have changed hugely as well. Many women have been freed from the daily grind of domestic labour with modern appliances, ready meals and child-minders. Weddings tend to be less about the bride leaving her family unit to join that of the groom and more about friends having fun in a party atmosphere. Divorce is quicker and easier, and remarriage, even multiple times, carries less stigma than it once did.

When we look at the changes to the floral arts themselves over time, we can see that the first flower arrangements were loose and open with no means of dividing or holding stems in place. This was followed by attempts to secure a design with small twigs wedged inside vases, an idea brought over from Japan. Sand and moss were then used in the same way by the Victorians, but designs were still natural and flowing. Wedding boughs carried over the bride's head, or secured to the gates of the church, were loose garlands of flowers and foliage, and there was no means of keeping the plant material fresh. Brides' bouquets were originally just a few tied stems of flowers; later bouquets were either bound with string and built up to form a handle or wired into a moss ball, a construction method thought to have been introduced to England by French maids.

Constance Spry (1886–1960), an English florist, laid the foundation for some of the traditional floristry we see today. Although many of the flowers Constance used were from the garden and the wild, which grew in a natural, unwieldy manner, good advice on lines, colour, proportion and form were given and published in her many books over the years. During this period, crumpled chicken wire or pin holders 'Kazan's' were used inside vases and containers to hold stems in position.

When flower production started again after the lull of the war, flowers were cultivated with straighter stems, making them easier to box and send to market. The ubiquity of the telephone now made possible an international system for sending flowers, and the need to standardize arrangements grew. Meanwhile, the development of floral foam made the precise positioning of flowers easier. Arrangements and wedding bouquets took on a rather stiff, unnatural look, but were uniform and easy for the florist to copy.

Styles of wedding bouquets and headdresses have been repeated down the centuries; it is mainly the method of construction that has changed. Modern flowers, of course, are larger hybridized versions of the original species and although lilies have fallen out of fashion for weddings at the time of writing, the one flower that has endured throughout time is the rose. The rose has been used for weddings both to decorate venues and in bouquets in every century. Wars, religion, economic and social change, and technological advances have influenced our choices of flowers, containers, the places we choose for weddings and styles of dresses. Today we are conscious of greenhouse gases and air pollution and now seek out local flower growers, not only for economy or environmental reasons but to source those endearing English country flowers with graciously bent stems. We have turned back the time on flowers standing straight, favouring the natural curvaceous flowing stems of the past!

2016: the hand-tied bouquet of today.

Chapter 2

The Practicalities of Organizing Wedding Flowers

A wedding is one of the most exciting celebrations a couple will plan together; therefore it is important that the couple is put at ease during any consultation. A meeting with the couple should be arranged as early as possible so that any suggestions can be worked through. For example, it is important to determine the size of the wedding, as this will indicate how much work there is to undertake. Finances, religion and lifestyle will also influence decisions. An assessment of the couple's ideas, hobbies, and colour scheme can be recorded to help identify the floral themes of the wedding. These themes may incorporate sentimental heritage and geographical ideas, for example, using *Moluccella laevis* 'bells of Ireland' for an Irish bride, groom or family connection, thistle for a Scottish connection or a unique rose for an English connection.

Further inspiration can be taken from the bride's dress, so ask for a picture and discuss the colour, shape, style and texture of the dress with a view to finding complementary flowers. If required, a mock bouquet can be made in advance to ensure the bride feels comfortable on her special day. During this initial meeting everyone must feel a connection so that creative, unique, stunning displays can be created for the happy couple.

Mood Boards

Mood boards are a fun way to help identify key flowers and communicate ideas. They can help your clients visualize the overall look you're trying to achieve and clarify key points. Creating two boards, one for the ceremony and one for the reception, is useful if the two venues have different themes. Mood boards should be created at the beginning of the planning process, but take into consideration the season in which the wedding is actually to take place. Flower choices for the correct time of year will have to be researched.

As well as flower pictures, fabrics, colour combinations, bridal party dresses and other wedding party outfits can be added to the board to help co-ordinate the floral choices. Cuttings from magazines of venues and their interiors help create the mood and stimulate other ideas. As the board begins to fill up you will be able to see at a glance if all the elements are harmonious. Add new ideas and discard old ones until all the final pieces fit into the mood and theme of the wedding.

Mood board.

Anglican Church Weddings

Anglican Church Locations

When planning church flowers, there are many considerations, such as size, style and location of the church. Floral decorations should be in proportion to the building and space they are to occupy, they should complement the period of the church, and be in keeping

LEFT: Country house 'The Mews'.

with its surroundings. Flower arrangements should not obscure any interesting architecture, ancient features or memorials.

COUNTRY CHURCHES (ANGLO-SAXON PERIOD)

These are small, simple churches built from stone, usually with one porch, a nave and chancel with small windows and doors set into their very thick walls and one aisle. There is very little space to arrange flowers without impeding the congregation, but small earthenware pots of flowers set on windowsills and simple arrangements of seasonal flowers outside the porch that harmonize with the building and countryside would be in keeping.

CATHEDRALS AND LARGE CHURCHES

Grand inner-city buildings will need large, bold floral arrangements for impact, and contemporary designs are more in keeping with the simplicity of modern architecture in newer buildings. To force a preconceived wedding theme into a venue without being sympathetic to the surroundings will result in loss of atmosphere and effect.

Lychgates are a beautiful and colourful statement to welcome any bride.

Church Decoration Areas

OUTSIDE THE CHURCH

Decorated lynch gates and floral archways can create a stunning first impression and will set the scene, perfect photo opportunities! These are a large undertaking and must be planned weeks in advance and require several helpers.

INSIDE THE CHURCH

The porch or other vestibules are good locations for floral designs provided access is not impeded. If the font is a

The porch of a church, a place for the bride to compose herself before being greeted by the vicar.

Stone side-seats inside the church porch with baskets of summer flowers.

prominent feature near the entrance and the architecture is conducive to decorating without obscuring any details, then this makes a welcoming display. The aisles can be transformed into a floral avenue, but take care you leave enough room for people to pass comfortably without knocking into the flowers.

The aisle leads to the chancel steps where the bride and groom take their vows, so this area will attract the most attention. Pedestal arrangements either side of the couple will frame and highlight the space and become a total part of the scene. As the ceremony is conducted standing up, the floral displays have to be tall enough to be seen over the heads of the congregation. A rood screen or choir screen could be decorated, but take care not to damage any stone or delicate woodcarving and keep the decorations lightweight.

Church windows are usually placed high to prevent worshippers from looking out and being distracted; however, flowers placed here should not block out any decorative stained glass. If a guest speaker has been asked to do a reading from the pulpit or lectern, flowers around the edge enhance this focal area, but make sure the speaker can be seen over the top.

Church pillars are usually made from stone or marble and may not have a secure area on which to attach flowers. Nevertheless, these can provide a romantic feel with garlands of greenery or flowers draped around them, and are high enough to be enjoyed by everyone, whether sitting or standing.

Frontals on the altar and vestments are usually white, and if you are given permission for flower arrangements here, they must never be taller than the standing cross.

Catholic Weddings

The Catholic Church has over time changed many of its traditional practices. Nonetheless, no flowers are allowed on the main altar – only things necessary for the Eucharist can be placed here. Flowers can be placed beside the altar or at the back of the altar, if there is one. Nothing should obscure the altar – or what is happening on it – from the view of the congregation. A few Catholic churches follow an old rule that sanctuary flowers must be genuine, not artificial. These churches consider fresh or dried arrangements appropriate, but not silks. Temporary decorations that add to the meaning of the service are generally a welcome addition to the church, such as the use of corn, vegetables etc., say for the wedding of a local farmer. Beyond these guidelines, the church allows a certain amount of leeway to each priest to determine what is suitable for his particular church. Some priests are more conservative than others, and some churches, by their very design, impose artistic restrictions on what a florist can do in good taste.

Greek Weddings

For Greek wedding ceremonies, two very large candles are placed in a prominent position close to the bride and groom. The candles can be decorated with ribbons or light garlands of flowers attached with tape. Both bride and groom have garlands of flowers placed on their heads and tied together to signify their union.

Jewish Weddings

Jewish wedding ceremonies usually take place on a Sunday in a synagogue. The marriage takes place under a 'chuppah', a square canopy held up by poles on each corner, and sometimes covered in a

Myrtle and white roses neatly top the pulpit.

Avenue of summer flowers for the bride's procession down the aisle.

blue cloth. Flowers can cover the canopy, or garlands can be placed on its perimeter; sprays of flowers on each corner are the usual decorations. Other areas that can be decorated are the 'bimah' where the register is signed, a floral screen that is used to separate men and women, and the entrance. All flowers are normally moved to the reception after the ceremony. There will be restrictions on what day you can arrange the flowers and you must wear a headscarf.

Period Venues

Period venues usually have listed status, which means restrictions on decorating selected areas of historical interest. These restrictions vary from venue to venue, so areas suggested here as being suitable for decorating are general and may not be applicable to all. Make sure you contact the in-house events person for your client's venue to discuss restrictions ahead of time. Then visit the venue with the couple, armed with a tape measure and camera.

Flower arrangements, as ever, must be in proportion to all the areas that are to be decorated to ensure the right atmosphere, and although they can be dream settings, large palatial buildings will need copious flower arrangements to do justice to their grandeur. If a budget has to be considered concentrate only on the areas that will have the most impact: the entrance, reception area and dining tables.

Country manor houses and castles (for example, from the Tudor period) can have smaller and more intimate rooms with lower ceilings and wood panelling. A candle arrangement combined with flowers in deep rich colours, with textured leaves and berries, would be in keeping to complement tapestries, heavy oak furniture and beams. Check first if naked-flame candles can be used, otherwise the battery types can be just as effective and are longer-lasting.

Seventeenth- to nineteenth-century period houses may have long sweeping driveways leading to the front door. If they are to be approached through woodland, lamps, candles or hanging flower decorations lining the route can create a mystical atmosphere and a sense of anticipation. Grand pillars and porticoes over the front door can look austere; binding simple garlands of greenery around the columns looks romantic, and is an easy and relatively economical way to set the scene. Any flowers outside the door may be at the

Pedestals of twigs, summer roses and hydrangeas.

in and be a lasting memory on the way out. Large fireplaces look resplendent with floral displays both in the hearth and on the mantel, and if the bride were to make use of sweeping staircases, swags of flowers and greenery on the banisters would frame her grand entrance.

Marquees, Tents and Yurts

Weddings under canvas can be wonderfully unrestrained, creative and full of fun. A relaxed styling of flowers has become very popular, especially if the tents are situated on a farmer's fields, or in the bride's garden. Bales of straw used for seating are in keeping, or a mix and match of old tables and chairs for the vintage look. Wild-looking country flowers in old jugs, jam jars, milk churns or meadow boxes are a nice way to complete the setting.

Possible pitfalls for rural locations are: locating a water supply, uneven ground for floor-standing flower designs, the weather (heat, rain, wind and cold all pose problems) and slugs, snails, mice and squirrels, which can be a menace to any flowers left overnight! Tents closed up for any length of time in the heat can dehydrate flowers and foliage, leaving them sad and wilting. On the positive side, there may be unlimited access when it comes to setting up and dismantling floral displays and little risk of damaging property.

Pillar stand with a ring of roses around a tall obelisk protecting church candles.

Meadow box filled with summer flowers.

mercy of the elements and risk damage. If, however, this is a very sheltered position, urns with elaborate eye-catching arrangements can be installed to great effect. Photographers take advantage of any steps for grouped wedding snaps, so any floral display here would make a good backdrop. Large doors usually open into a great hall that may be highly decorated with marble pillars and floors. This would be a suitable area for large designs of blousy roses, peonies, hydrangea and soft, swirling foliage to welcome guests

Practicalities

Money Matters

It is recommended that at least 10 per cent of the overall cost of the wedding should be allocated to flowers. Underestimating the impact of flowers may affect the mood and atmosphere you want to convey, and the more you can allocate to the floral budget, the more varied your options will be. Careful wedding planning is essential to ensure finances will stretch to flower allocation. Priority has to be with the bride, where only the best quality of flowers will do, then the bridesmaids and groom, the reception (the place where you will spend the most time), then the church (or other ceremony venue) and, if finances allow, the wedding guests' buttonholes.

To save money, think about growing your own flowers. Sourcing garden foliage from family or a local farm that trades in 'pick your own' may also be an option. If the ceremony venue or church are separate from the reception venue you may wish to move flowers from one location to another to make the most of your displays, but please leave some complimentary flowers in the church, if you are using one, for Sunday service. Collect or buy some of the chosen flowers and practise a few arrangements well before the wedding. This will help you identify what will or will not work and enable you to quantify the overall amount of flowers needed. At this point you can adjust your flower budget accordingly and keep it in check. It may be expensive to purchase large pedestal stands, tall vases and candelabras if you are not going to make use of them again. To keep costs in check you can hire or borrow vases and stands, collect recycled glass jars and look in charity shops or on Internet auction sites.

Closer to the wedding, be aware that flower prices may fluctuate based on seasonality, weather conditions, availability and world events calendars (flowers are at a premium on Mother's Day, for example, and this date differs from country to country). Transport delays and supply and demand are all factors to be taken into account. There are some conditions that are simply out of your control so be prepared to adjust your allowance if necessary.

Time Management

When you have determined the total number of flowers needed to complete all the arrangements, a timed schedule for growing flowers from seed can be started. Plan for at least a year or longer in advance of the wedding!

Start by collecting buckets in which to condition the flowers and foliage, and then shop for all your sundries, vases and containers. This can be done well in advance, with the items then set aside. Decide on where you want to source the flowers, i.e., wholesalers, flower shops, supermarkets or pick your own.

Sourcing Flowers

The English countryside and our gardens have a wealth of flora and foliage available to the bride, and are a great source for seasonal inspiration. Recent inspiration has focused on a trend for flowers to look as if they have been freshly picked from the field. If this is what you are looking to do, be aware of the Wildlife and Countryside Act of 1981, as there are limits and restrictions on what you can pick, and remember to ask the landowner's permission if you are picking from private fields. With the rapid decline in English woodlands, wild meadows and hedgerows and the loss of many species, you should be mindful not to over-pick. Wild flowers certainly do complement yurt, tent and barn settings, but for the sake of conservation it is better to seek out English nurseries and farm growers for this purpose. They have a good selection of quality country flowers full of fragrance, including eco-friendly and sustainably produced varieties. Buying British also ensures a far greener carbon footprint for your flowers.

The local 'pick your own' growers sell small quantities of flowers by the bucket or bunch. Local flower markets are also a good source of supply and will stock many varieties that will help you compare prices as they import flowers from Holland and around the world. Some wholesalers also stock a certain amount of English flowers when in season and will give you help and advice if you visit when it is quiet after the big shop buyers have gone. But as wholesalers sell to the trade, their bunches of flowers contain many more stems than are needed, so may not be economical if you only require a small

Wholesale flower market.

Field of English country-farm flowers.

avoid the possibility of any spillage. Protect any ribboning on the handle from getting wet by wrapping it with cellophane. Insert the bouquet, taking care to bolster it up with tissue paper

Wrapped bucket, ready for a hand-tied bouquet.

amount. Florists can be a flexible source of supply as they will sell you anything from one flower to many. They can also help with your selection, give advice and have flowers that are already conditioned for you. Supermarkets have their own nurseries that supply them direct and have a good choice of Fairtrade flowers that are reasonably priced. There are also wholesalers and importers found on the Internet who will deliver flowers direct.

Packing and Delivery

After hours of preparation, the last thing you want is to ruin all your hard work with careless delivery practices. Small arrangements in floral foam can be delivered already made up, provided you have a suitable vehicle with a flat base. Large displays are best worked on *in situ*, therefore flowers and foliage are best packed in flat boxes or stable water

containers for the journey. Delicate flowers like lilies will need their open blooms supported and protected with tissue paper. Start packing non-perishable items the night before the arranging day, leaving enough space for the flowers. Have a checklist ready, as it will be time-consuming to go back if you have forgotten anything.

HAND-TIED BOUQUETS
Hand-tied bouquets can be delivered dry, or in water if the weather is hot and there is a long distance to travel. Select a bucket suitable in size for the bouquet to fit into easily without damaging any flowers. Dress the bucket in wrapping paper or cellophane. Select a container to fit inside the bucket that will hold only a small amount of water but is sufficient to take the stems of the bouquet. Firmly pack the inside edge of the bucket with paper pressing against the water container to hold it in place and thus

Bouquet inside a prepared bucket ready for delivery.

PROTECTION FOR WILD PLANTS AFFORDED BY THE WILDLIFE AND COUNTRYSIDE ACT, 1981

Section 13 identifies measures for the protection of wild plants. It prohibits the unauthorized intentional uprooting of any wild plant species and forbids any picking, uprooting or destruction of plants listed on Schedule 8. It also prohibits the sale, etc., or possession for the purpose of sale, of any plants on Schedule 8 or parts or derivatives of Schedule 8 plants. It provides certain defences, e.g. provision to cover incidental actions that are an unavoidable result of an otherwise lawful activity.

Note that it is not normally an offence to pick the 'Four Fs': Fruit, Foliage, Fungi or Flowers – assuming that none of them are protected specifically – which are growing wild if they are for personal use and not for sale. This is not part of the Act but a part of common law. It covers such customs as blackberry picking, taking ivy and holly at Christmas, mushroom-hunting and gathering sloes.

To exercise this right you must be somewhere you have a legal right to be – such as on a public footpath or in a public park. You cannot just go anywhere and pick the Four Fs. Obviously if enough people exercise this right at the same time and in the same place it could cause a lot of damage to habitats and species. In some places such as parks or commons, local byelaws prevent such activities.

Section 13

Part 1 (a) intentional picking, uprooting or destruction of plants on Schedule 8.
Part 1 (b) unauthorized intentional uprooting of any wild plant not included in Schedule 8.
Part 2 (a) selling, offering for sale, possessing or transporting for purpose of sale, any plants (live or dead, part or derivative) on Schedule 8.
 Part 2 (b) advertising for buying or selling such things.

The following is a short list of the most common plants and flowers that you may recognize in the English countryside. You can also find the full list on the website.

Common Name	Scientific Name
Small Alison	*Alyssum alyssoides*
Bluebell	*Hyacinthoides non-scripta*
Wild Cotoneaster	*Cotoneaster integerrimus*
Sand crocus	*Romulea columnae*
Dickie's bladder fern	*Cystopteris dickieana*
Killarney fern	*Trichomanes speciosum*
Alpine gentian	*Gentiana nivalis*
Dune gentian	*Gentianella uliginosa*
Early gentian	*Gentianella anglica*
Fringed gentian	*Gentianella ciliata*
Spring gentian	*Gentiana verna*
Wild Gladiolus	*Gladiolus illyricus*
Stinking goosefoot	*Chenopodium vulvaria*
Red helleborine	*Cephalanthera rubra*
Young's helleborine	*Epipactis youngiana*
Alpine sulphur-tresses	*Alectoria ochroleuca*
Snowdon lily	*Lloydia serotina*
Cambridge milk-parsley moss	*Selinum carvifolia*
Early spider orchid	*Ophrys sphegodes*
Fen orchid	*Liparis loeselii*
Ghost orchid	*Epipogium aphyllum*
Lapland marsh orchid	*Dactylorhiza lapponica*
Late spider orchid	*Ophrys fuciflora*
Lizard orchid	*Himantoglossum hircinum*
Military orchid	*Orchis militaris*
Monkey orchid	*Orchis simia*
Plymouth pear	*Pyrus cordata*
Alpine moss	*Pertusaria bryontha*
Ground pine	*Ajuga chamaepitys*
Cheddar pink	*Dianthus gratianopolitanus*
Deptford pink	*Dianthus armeria*
Whorled Solomon's seal	*Polygonatum verticillatum*
Early star-of-Bethlehem	*Gagea bohemica*
Fen violet	*Viola persicifolia*
Field wormwood	*Artemisia campestris*

under and around the edges of the flowers. Give it one last misting of water if necessary. Hand-tied sheaf bouquets can be packed in the same way but with additional tissue paper to support the back. Label and add a bow for presentation, white for the bride with colour-coordinated ribbons for the bridesmaids, with names clearly visible and secured to the box.

POMANDERS
Measure the finished length of the pomander including its ribbon handle and select a box large enough to

Wrapped box suitable for packing pomanders.

accommodate the whole length with a little extra in depth. This extra space will prevent the bottom flowers from potential damage. Cover the box with wrapping paper and pack the bottom of the box with tissue paper. Thread the ribbon handle of the pomander over a stick that is strong enough to carry the weight of the pomander, and long enough to balance diagonally across the top of the box. Dangle the pomander in the centre of the box and tie ribbon bows on each end of the supporting stick and tie around the perimeter of the box under the flaps. This will keep the pomander secure and prevent it from slipping. Finally, pack more tissue gently around the pomander to stop it swinging from side to side and damaging the flowers, then mist with water and label the box.

HEADDRESSES, CORSAGES AND BUTTONHOLES
Headdresses, corsages and buttonholes should be presented in flat boxes. Select boxes of a suitable size to fit all the buttonholes, cover them with wrapping paper and line with tissue, leaving enough that you can scrunch some tissue up and divide and support the flowers with it. Mist the flowers and cover the boxes with cellophane, then

secure with tape. Label each box clearly: Groom, Best Man, Ushers, Mother of the Bride etc. Bridesmaids' circlets may differ in size so naming boxes individually will avoid any confusion and give a personal touch.

Tip: Adding a few extra pins to buttonhole boxes will alleviate any problems with pins being misplaced by nervous hands!

THE BRIDE'S SHOWER BOUQUET
Choose a box that is large enough to hold the length and width of the bouquet, with a little extra space for packing material around the edge. Wrap the box with decorative paper. Secure four garden sticks at the top end of the box. These should be evenly spaced and high enough to support a cellophane covering that will protect the profile of the bouquet. Line the box with scrunched-up tissue paper, taking care to add extra at the point where the handle of the bouquet is to be packed. Once the bouquet is carefully laid in the box, extra tissue can be used for support in and around delicate flowers if needed. Mist the bouquet with water and cover the box with cellophane, leaving extra height over the garden sticks.

Prepared box with pomander inside ready for delivery.

Boxes prepared ready for buttonholes, headdresses and corsages.

Box of buttonholes.

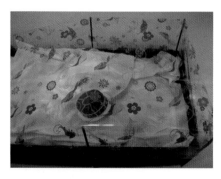

Shower bouquet box showing position of the bouquet handle.

Checklist for Arranging and Dismantling Floral Displays in the Venue

- Have you informed the venue events manager, vicar or church flower-arrangers ahead of time about planned floral displays? Compromises may have to be made.
- If you are working *in situ*, is there is a spare room that you can use to store or assemble the flowers?
- Is there another event after your wedding? How quickly do the flowers have to be cleared away?
- Can you use church or venue containers or pedestal stands and do they have stepladders if you need them?
- Are all arrangements stable, clear of pathways and visible to the guests?
- Do you know where to find the water supply? Some rural churches may not be connected to the mains and you may have to bring your own water.
- Do you have waterproof sheets to protect the floor and brushes to clean up?
- Is there a waste tip you can make use of? If not, take away all your rubbish and recycle any greenery.
- Who is responsible for dismantling and clearing flowers away?
- Have you checked the lighting? Some flowers do not show up as well

as others under certain lights.
- Is confetti permitted at the venue?
- Are there any festivals, monuments or restrictions to be aware of?
- If the church or venue is kept locked, who is the key-holder and will they open early for you, or let you stay late?
- Are there any special meetings, services or choir practice in the venue?
- If your venue is a church, funerals can happen at the last minute; will your wedding flowers be appropriated if left in place?
- Do you have consent to use screws or nails in the fabric of the venue? Previous damage caused by carelessness may mean the venue no longer allows arrangements needing these fixtures.
- Have you taken care to protect surfaces from water damage? Remember you will need to clean up after each arrangement.
- Have you taken note of any parking restrictions at the venue?

Hints and tips

- It is courteous to leave some flowers for Sunday service if your venue is a church, but remember that flowers on pew ends are always removed.
- The bride and groom may like to distribute the flowers among the guests after the wedding. This also saves on the task of clearing them away.
- If there is another wedding at the venue on the same day, your clients might consider liaising with the other couple to share costs and use mutually suitable colours.

Countdown to the Wedding

Make sure you have a checklist ready, as adrenaline will be running high and

time management will be critical. One week before the wedding, contact the venue(s) to confirm all your agreed arrangements, and check that there are no alterations or hiccups.

Four Days in Advance

Wrap all boxes ready for delivering buttonholes and bouquets, and prepare the containers requiring floral foam, then set these aside. If you are foraging for flowers keep an eye on their availability. If bad weather has caused damage you may have to buy extra flowers to make up the shortfall.

Three Days in Advance

Source the flowers and condition them. For example, lilies will require at least four or more days to open if they are in tight bud (see Chapter 5 for further details on specific varieties).

Two Days in Advance

Larger church or reception flowers can be assembled in advance. If preparation on site is possible, careful transportation of flowers is essential to keep them undamaged and well hydrated. Other small table posies can be made up in advance and stored in a cool place, or delivered to the venue with prior consent.

One Day in Advance

If there are any hand-tied bouquets, these can be made up first and stored in water in a cool place. All other wired designs, buttonholes, corsages and the bride's bouquet can be made the evening before or early on the morning of the wedding. The weather and your storage facilities will dictate the timing.

The Wedding Day

Delivering the bride's, bridesmaids', and father and mother of the bride's flowers punctually, at the prearranged hour, will put the bride's mind at rest. The bridal flowers are the last element of the wedding to be delivered, so will complete the months of planning. Once they arrive, the bride can feel confident, relaxed and enjoy the day. (Traditionally, if you are delivering flowers for a Greek wedding, the groom presents his bride with her bouquet so you may have to deliver to his address first.) Show the bride how to take the bouquet out of the box and demonstrate how to hold it. If the bouquet is hand-tied and has wet stems, take a towel or kitchen paper and thoroughly wipe away any water from the handle before passing to the bride. The bride should be allowed to hold the bouquet for reassurance and be asked to check all the other bouquets and buttonholes over before you leave. The groom's, best man's, ushers', and groom's parents' buttonholes may be delivered to a house, the wedding ceremony venue, or a local hotel. Give instructions on how to pin in the groom's buttonhole, and how to attach any corsages (see Chapter 6).

Tip: It is a good idea to take a workbox with you just in case anything needs attention or an extra buttonhole is required at the last minute. Personal service is always appreciated.

Themes

Today, wedding venues being granted a license are diverse, such as football stadiums, cemeteries, beaches, piers and the zoo. Registrars are asked to perform ceremonies while skydiving and underwater, and wedding 'themes' have become the norm. Themes can be personal to each couple and may be inspired by their interests, hobbies,

Beach wedding – the young bridesmaid has a bucket filled with sea holly, seashells, starfish, brunia (looks like pebbles) coral celosia, coral roses and grey moss.

Bridesmaid's Alice-band headdress with sea holly, seashells, coral roses and grey moss.

Bucket and hand-tied bouquets with coral roses, coral celosia, sea holly, grey moss, brunia and beige dried seaweed.

Long glass-vase table decoration filled with sand, pebbles, seashells, starfish, sea holly, coral celosia, dried beige seaweed, brunia and grey moss.

Groom's buttonhole of sea holly and seashells with a pearl buttonhole pin.

popular events, unusual wedding venues and wanting to be different. They can be exciting, extraordinary and stretch your creative imagination.

A beach wedding theme, like the one pictured here, might be interpreted with sea holly, coral fern and natural dried seaweed, coral colours matched with roses, celosia (which resembles sea coral), and brunia flower heads looking like pebbles. Accessories like seashells, starfish, sand and pearl-headed buttonhole pins could all help to set the scene.

If you are not familiar with the many plants and flowers available to help you interpret a theme, a job like this may take some research, but if carried out well can be most rewarding.

Settings can also be given a period makeover and the theme can be carried through the location, the flowers and the style of dress. Today's wedding celebrations are all about having fun!

Trends

Trends evolve and flow, influenced by our daily lives. In the eighties, brides followed the trend of flouncy 'meringue' dresses and large trailing shower bouquets like Princess Diana's. Now, new celebrities, pop stars, models and other rich and famous people influence trends with their huge followings. Celebrity-inspired weddings are the easiest to plan as the styles and arrangements are splashed all over the media, but they are much less of a creative challenge. To prevent the new bride copying the same flowers, the same setting, and the same colours, it would be more creative for the florist to suggest something different that will make the bride stand out from the crowd. The 'all the fun at the fair' wedding pictured here themed every guests' table by the games found at a fair: 'tug of war', 'splat the rat' etc. The names of flowers could not be used to interpret the games but there was an opportunity to create ice cream tubs and bowls, and tall candyfloss stands of flowers for the top table, each stand using twenty-five stems of hydrangea and twenty-five stems of pink gypsophila, to interpret some of the treats synonymous with fairs.

Ice-cream bowl filled with floral foam sprinkled with spray roses and drizzled with angel vine.

Top table, with a line of ice-cream tubs, cupcakes and two (only one shown) very large stands of candyfloss.

Ice-cream bowl, small ice-cream tub and summer-flower cupcakes.

Guests' table, with enough flower cupcakes for each guest to take one home.

Chapter 3

Choosing Flowers

On a daily basis we do not tend to take a great deal of notice of the colours that surround us; plants in the garden, hedgerows, trees, décor in our homes and offices. It is often only when we arrange a wedding and choose bridesmaids' dresses, for example, that we become more conscious of colour. For some brides, the colour for their attendants' clothing is a forgone conclusion, innate years before any plans are announced. For others, the choice is overwhelming and it may not now be just the bride's choice but the choice of overenthusiastic bridesmaids as well.

The relationship between the colour of the dresses and the colour of the flowers is very important; they must work together to achieve a harmonious relationship. Brightly coloured dresses work best with some equally bright flowers, while subtly coloured flowers may be overpowered by bright dress material. Tones of sage and mint green with closely matched flowers may create an understatement and be lost against the dress, but by using a medley of colours, including the greens of the dress, you will bring life to the overall look. Whatever is decided, make sure that the flowers complement and are

Colour wheel of flowers.

compatible with the complexions, skin tone and hair colours of all the bridesmaids and bride.

Looking at the colour wheel and the many harmonies that can be achieved will help you to choose colours that evoke the mood of the wedding. However, this can only be a guide as,

with many colours, there is variation when in print and our perception of colour can also differ from person to person. So comparing swatches of material against flowers in the daylight is advisable. Seeing colour is also a lot more than just a visual activity. The psychological aspect can stimulate our

LEFT: Polychromatic colours.

Primary colours: red, blue, yellow.

There are also three secondary colours: violet, green and orange.

By mixing a primary colour with an adjacent secondary colour, we get six tertiary colours: red-violet, red-orange, yellow-orange, yellow-green, blue-green and blue-violet.

Triadic colours: created by the use of three colours equidistant on the wheel.

Triadic colours: lemon, pink and powder blue.

Polychromatic colours: created by the use of many colours together.

Polychromatic colours: many colours together.

Complementary colours: created by the use of two colours opposite or approximately opposite each other on the colour wheel.

Analogous colours: created when using two, three or four colours next to each other on the wheel.

senses and evoke all kinds of emotions, so colour is an important element of any wedding. Bouquets and floral designs with clear, radiant colours are lively, cheerful and stimulate the senses, whilst arrangements in pastel-coloured, mixed tones create a more subdued, elegant and passive mood or reserved and dreamy atmosphere.

There are twelve colours around the wheel. Yellow, yellow-orange, orange, red-orange, red, red-violet, violet, blue-violet, blue, blue-green, green, yellow-green.

There are three primary colours: red, yellow and blue.

Secondary colours: orange, green, violet.

Analogous colours: three or four colours next to each other on the colour wheel.

Monochromatic colour: the use of tints, tones and shades of all one colour; such a close colour harmony can become monotonous unless textural contrasts and varying extremes of colour value can be added to create interest.

Monochromatic colours: tints, tones and shades of one colour.

Tints, tones and shades: by adding white to any colour, a tint or pastel colour is achieved. By adding black to a colour we get a shade of colour. Finally, by adding grey to a colour we get a tone

Tints, tones and shades of colours.

Pastel tints of colours.

of colour. To demonstrate how tints (pastels), tones and shades can be achieved in a bouquet, the following pictures show possible combinations of flowers and foliage.

The combination of flowers in this hand-tied bouquet demonstrate extremes of colour. Cosmos 'chocolate' is one of the deepest shades, where the flowers are almost black. This is mixed with a pink rose that is tinted almost white and toned with *Scabiosa stellata* and *Leycesteria*. As you can see, colour can be used in a fascinating way to create atmosphere and interpret the loveliest and most romantic moods for a wedding.

Red

The colour red is associated with love and passion in many places around the world. The rose ties both concepts

together and is used extensively for weddings on Valentine's Day. The colour can vary from the brightest pillbox red to the deepest almost black red, but the message is the same. Red is associated with luxury, richness, excitement and heat, but can also be harsh and spell danger. This colour may be too hot for a sweltering summer wedding, but would warm up a wedding in the midst of winter.

Pink

The associations linked to soft, delicate pink are tenderness, charm and innocence. Childlike, sweet and feminine, peonies and roses spring to mind. Shocking or fuchsia pink, as seen in many gerberas, on the other hand, sends a strong, lively signal for a bride who is young at heart.

Blue

Blue, as the colour of the sky, can stand for distance and space, serenity and tranquillity. When linked to water or the sea, coolness and calm can be conveyed. Blue symbolizes freshness, loyalty and friendship. It is a refreshing, cooling colour for hot summer weddings but can leave you cold in the middle of winter.

Green

Green has a sense of calm and conveys freshness and youthful vitality. It is the colour of nature and therefore rejuvenation, hope and healing. Some greens are chosen for bridesmaids' dresses as the colour can be viewed as neutral, and can therefore be juxtaposed with many floral colour combinations.

Yellow

Yellow is a refreshing colour that shines and enlivens; it is associated with springtime, the sun, cheerfulness and optimism. This bright colour dances with delight when used alongside grassy banks of daffodils in the early part of the year, but may well look out of place for a winter wedding. Yellow is the most luminous colour on the wheel and will show up in any lighting.

Orange

Orange can be linked with the sun and therefore has a cheering, stimulating, activating effect. It is also an autumnal colour, signalling warmth and earthiness. This is a natural colour for autumn weddings if you match orange berries and tints and tones of autumn leaves to the theme.

Peach

Soft, feminine, soothing and gentle, peach looks good in spring teamed with cream and buttery lemon, in summer with baby blue and in autumn when mixed with a medley of autumn foliage and berries.

White

White stands for innocence, chastity and purity, and has therefore long been associated with brides. It is the colour of perfection and cleanliness. Using white in floral designs and bouquets can sometimes be harsh, with white flowers standing out like blobs if not used with other tints and tones to blend them in. 'White' roses vary, some with tints of pink, or lemon, and some with tones of beige, or metallic tones. There are many varieties and one for each of the many white, ivory, champagne and cream shades of bridal dresses.

Gold

This colour is noble, exclusive, magnificent and suggests perfection. There are no flowers that are actually gold, and the ones closest to the colour tend to look a little eggy yellow. It is best to add gold with accessories to introduce this colour into a theme.

Silver

Cool and sophisticated, silver may also indicate something temporary. There are silver/grey leaves that can highlight the colour in *Ceropegia gardneri* and *Tillandsia*. Or you might try turning some leaves over and using the undersides, *Elaeagnus* and *Garrya elliptica* are good options for this.

Violet/Purple

As the colour of dignity and contemplation, purple stands for preparation and transition. Violet stands for mysticism and magic, but also royalty, luxury and fantasy. Some brides refer to this purple as Cadbury's chocolate purple, which the purple lisys matches perfectly.

'White' flowers.

Grey

Grey is associated with age and grey foliage is often used to interpret vintage or winter weddings. It is also a neutral colour. Senecio, brunia and the air plant ceropegia are just a few good choices for grey floral art.

Artificial Lighting

Some types of artificial lighting may change or interfere with the colours of your flowers, so do keep this in mind when planning with your clients.

Fluorescent Strip Lighting

Most fluorescent strip lighting, installed in many local authority halls (which are often hired for weddings), is really bad for deep red roses, carnations and gerberas, leaving them looking muddy brown and creating an optical illusion of apparent holes in an arrangement. This perception of a change of colour is because fluorescent light has a blue/green cast. Blue delphiniums and irises will be enhanced and glow under this lighting, while daffodils and sunflowers will appear to have a slight greenish tinge.

Mercury Lights

Mercury bulbs emit light with a violet/blue/green bias, causing reds to appear dull. This type of bulb is also prone to dimming with age, further reducing the light level.

Halogen Lights

The wavelength of light produced by halogen bulbs are very close to that of natural sunlight so any colour will look good in these conditions.

Tungsten Lights

Tungsten bulbs used in ordinary household fittings give out light with a warm orange/red bias. This enhances red as well as orange shades and can make some yellows quite vivid. Blues and purples, which are receding colours under normal daylight conditions, become dull and grey. Blue delphiniums, scabious and iris viewed from a distance in a church or large hall will fade into the background under tungsten light.

Sodium Lights

High-pressure sodium lighting is often used in exhibition halls. Although it has a high yellow/green output, it emits some light in most wavelengths. Its yellow light sucks the vibrancy from pinks and burgundies but maximizes the effect of yellow-splashed leaves like aucuba and euonymus.

Tip: Light tints and bright pinks show up well in all types of lighting, though tones of pink may look slightly grey.

Style

The appropriate style and shape of a bouquet will be dependent on the design and fabric of the bride's dress, the height and size of the bride and the theme of the wedding. It will not look in proportion if the bride chooses an enormous bouquet if she is 4'9" (1m 45cm) tall, and rather plump; nor is a tiny Victorian posy wise if she is 5'10" (1m 78cm) and very slim.

The right bouquet can accentuate a tiny waist or disguise a thick one. When a bride first emerges from the front door of her house, first we notice how beautiful she looks, then our eye naturally follows down to the bodice of her dress as this is usually where most detailing can be seen. The gaze then follows down to her waist, as this is where a bouquet is normally held, then down to the hem of her dress. To keep the eye's movement fluid the bouquet should not interrupt the flow with over-dominant flowers.

Suggested designs are just that; a bride may choose a style just because she likes it, or she may be restricted by the budget. But to give a bride with round hips a round bouquet will just emphasize the obvious. Large, blousy and full-skirted dresses suit an equally large bouquet, maybe a waterfall, shower or cascading style caressing the front of the skirt. For a tailored dress nipped in at the waist with a medium skirt, a smaller, neater teardrop style may suit better. Slim-line dresses made from lace, chiffon, silk crêpe or similar materials that fall softly over the body with a freedom of movement look best with a long, slim, graceful flow of plant material, kept well within the width of the bride's hips. Short, 1950s-style dresses suit a small, cheeky hand-tied bouquet, handbag or novelty design, or for a full, swinging skirt it is the fashion to hold a fuller 'Rococo' bunch. When Sarah Ferguson married Prince Andrew, her bouquet of lily-of-the-valley, lilies, small lemon roses and gardenias was wired very neatly into an S for Sarah shape, otherwise known as the 'Hogarth curve', which suited her very neat, fitted wedding dress.

Texture

Once the shape of the bouquet has been decided upon another element to consider is the texture of the dress. Texture is the surface area of the fabric and plays just as important a role as colour, style and so on. A dress that has a dull texture, like silk dupion or raw silk, may look very flat if highlighted with very shiny flowers, anthuriums for example, or shiny leaves, and if the

TABLE 1. FABRICS AND COMPLEMENTARY FLOWERS

Material	Texture	Flower
Brocade	Heavy, embossed, patterned	Roses, carnations, berries, *Celosia*, peonies, hydrangea
Chiffon	Lightweight, plain, woven, sheer	*Astilbe*, orchids, sweetpea, lilly-of-the-valley
Cotton	Ranges from medium to heavy	Daisies, astrantia, *Ammi*, scabious, feverfew
Crêpe-de-Chine	Heavy and rough	Arum lilies, gardenias, Eucharist lilies
Lace	Patterned	Orchids, lily-of-the-valley, roses, stephanotis
Organdy	Light, fine and translucent	Peonies, English country roses, sweetpea, scabious, larkspur
Satin	Ranges from matte to shiny	Matte texture – roses, arum lilies, gardenias. Shiny texture – anthuriums, tulips, lilies.
Silk dupion	Light and matte	Freesias, orchids, roses, Easter lilies

bride's dress is shiny, using dull-textured flowers like arum lilies or grey foliage may make the flowers look lifeless or flat. Brides with impaired vision may welcome a mix of flowers and foliage with texture for extra sensory perception. Full-length lace dresses may need flowers with a stronger outline to help them show up against the patterned material.

Flower Meanings (Floriography)

No flower's name is without meaning so it is possible to incorporate a variety of very personal meanings within a bride's bouquet. Some meanings differ from country to country so be sure the interpretation you aim to use is universal (or at least correct for the background of your client and their guests) otherwise have quite a different effect to the one you intended!

Floriography can be quite a fun way to build up a bouquet even if only the nurseryman's name of a flower is used: every single commercially grown flower has its own name. Another easy option would be to use flowers to signify the bride's, groom's or a family nationality. The rose represents England and the United States of America but you could go deeper by using the flower of the county or state from which the bride or groom originates. Shamrock or 'Paddy's Pride Ivy' can be used for an Irish bride and daffodils can be selected for a bride or groom with Welsh heritage. Bringing the groom's nationality into the mix adds further interest and a union of both parties. Look at old photographs of the bride's mother's bouquet or even grandmother's bouquet, if sentimentality is to be incorporated. This is particularly poignant if the mother or grandmother cannot attend the wedding.

Commercial names for flowers can also be incorporated into the bouquet. There are thousands of names given to flowers and these are constantly being updated when a new variety is developed. However, there are steadfast varieties that have long borne the same name. Table 2, is a useful guide to popular flower meanings, and this book's index also contains a web link to a more comprehensive list).

Perfume

Choosing perfumed flowers will enrich and enliven a bouquet, so scent is just as important an element to consider as colour, texture and shape. For brides with impaired vision, perfume plays a major role when selecting blooms. On first opening the bouquet box, the bride will be greeted by the most intoxicating perfume; this might start the heart racing and stimulate romantic feelings, as it has done through the centuries. For some, it is a must to include fragrant flowers, so the bride can waft down the

TABLE 2. FLORIOGRAPHY AND SCENTED BLOOMS USED IN THIS BOOK

Flower	Meaning	Scent
Anigozanthos	Kangaroo paws	n/a
Anemone	Forsaken	n/a
Bluebell	Constancy	Light
Butterfly orchid	Gaiety	n/a
Caustis	Koala fern	n/a
Carnation, pink	Woman's love	Faint spice
Clematis	Cognitive beauty	n/a
Chrysanthemum	I love	Organic
Eucharist lily	Maiden charms	Medium sweet
Forget-me-not	Don't forget me!	n/a
Heather	Good luck	Faint
Honesty	Honesty	n/a
Honeysuckle	Devoted affection	Medium sweet
Hyacinth	Sporty and playful	Strong
Hydrangea	Heartlessness	n/a
Jasmine	Grace and elegance	Medium sweet
Larkspur, white	Levity	n/a
Lilac, purple	First love	Medium
Lily-of-the-valley	To be happy again	Faint sweet
Mint	Virtue	Strong minty
Myrtle	Love	Medium/strong sweet
Narcissus	Egotism	Medium
Orchid	Beauty	n/a
Peony	Shame, bashfulness	n/a
Rose, red, Naomi	Love	Medium
Rose, white, Avalanche	Purity	n/a
Rose, David Austin	Juliet	Light tea
Rose, single	Simplicity	Faint
Rosemary	Remembrance	Medium/strong
Scabious	Unfortunate love	n/a
Snowdrop	Hope	n/a
Solomon's seal	Concealment	n/a
Stock	Lasting beauty	Strong musk
Tulip	Declaration of love	n/a

smelling fresh flowers and herbs. Some perfumes are heavy and overbearing while others are delicate and sweet; other leaves and herbs can be refreshingly aromatic, or astringent. You must also remember that what the olfactory system receives and translates into smells varies from person to person, so scent is an entirely personal choice and what appeals to one may be a repugnant odour to another. Make sure your clients are happy with the floral scents you plan to use before arrangements are finalized.

While lily-of-the-valley and stephanotis may be the ideal flowers for the bride who prefers a perfumed bouquet, they will need wiring. Lily-of-the-valley, with its delicate sprays of tiny, bell-shaped flowers, takes nimble fingers to wind silver wire down the length of its stems to make it hold up against wilting. Once cut, these flowers won't last long. Stephanotis, meanwhile, has waxy, star-shaped flowers that can be cut off the main stem and wired individually for headdresses, corsages and to form trails in shower bouquets. These little blossoms will last nearly a week out of water and smell delicious.

Scented lily-of-the-valley bouquet.

aisle leaving a puff of perfume in her wake, but for those with hay fever, perfumed flowers must be avoided if there is to be a dry eye while vows are being pledged.

It is understandable that you may want to take every chance to use scented flowers in arrangements in the venue or to fill a room with perfumed flowers, and there is nothing nicer than beautiful flowers imparting their delicious scent. But selecting a suitable flower with an agreeable perfume can only be done in the flesh; pictures and descriptive interpretations of various scents will not replace the personal experience of

Chapter 4

Tools, Equipment and Containers

For you to achieve successful floral design pieces you will need good-quality tools and materials. The most important tools are some good cutting implements. All tools with a blade should be kept clean, sharp, well maintained and stored out of reach of young children, preferably in a toolbox. Over time you will build up a selection of containers, which should be washed after use and stored safely. Glass vases and jars become slippery in wet hands, and are best stored in boxes and out of harm's way. If you decide to buy floral foam in bulk and store it, it should never be placed on a top shelf as this may lead to the dust from the foam getting into your eyes when reaching up. Large pedestal stands should be checked for stability after each use, as metal legs can sometimes become damaged, uneven and lose stability. Rustic containers and wooden creates can look attractive but may cause snagging if rough surfaces are left unattended. A little light sanding will sort out any splintering. Baskets with plastic liners, and metal and ceramic containers should always be tested for water seepage before use. Note that unglazed terracotta can last a few hours before you discover it is porous and it leaks all over the white top-tablecloth!

LEFT: Urns and containers.

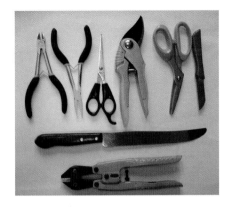

Scissors, knives, secateurs, wire-cutters.

Cutting Tools

Scissors and Secateurs

Flower scissors are used for cutting soft to medium stems of flowers and plant material. When choosing scissors, try before you buy: ask to hold them to gauge that the finger and thumb position is suitable for your grip. Many outlets also sell left-handed scissors. Ribbon scissors are used for cutting ribbons and fabrics without tearing the material. These small scissors are lightweight and sharp. Secateurs are strong tools used for heavy, woody and thick stems. There is only one blade, which closes against a flat surface.

Floristry Knives

These small knives may come with a straight blade, a curved blade or blades that retract into a handle. They are very sharp and give a good, clean cut through soft and medium stems. A long-bladed floristry knife can be used for cutting through floral foam.

Wire-Cutters and Pliers

There are various grades of wire-cutter, including heavy-duty, medium-duty and lightweight options. Choose wire-cutters appropriate to the thickness of your wire – the aim is to cut without having to twist and damage the blade. A clean cut will ensure that you leave no potentially snagging rough edges. Pliers are used for twisting, holding and bending wires; they can have a blunt or round nose.

Wire

Wires that come in sets of pre-measured lengths and thicknesses are called 'stub' wires. Wires that can be wound on a roll are called 'reel' wires, and can be covered in paper, plastic or a green lacquer coating. Fine galvanized silver wires are known as 'rose' wires. To keep wires from premature rusting, wrap and store in a dry place.

Reel Wire

Reel wires are used to bind and secure materials together and come in thicknesses of 24swg (0.56mm), called mossing wire, and 36–28swg (0.20–0.38mm), known as binding wire.

Decorative Wire

Aluminium wires are malleable and allow you to mould them into shapes useful for supporting flowers and adding interest when creating wedding designs including bouquets, corsages, and buttonholes. They come in a large variety of colours. Bullion and myrtle

Stub Wire	
Imperial gauge (standard wire gauge)	Metric gauge (millimetres)
15swg	1.80mm
18swg	1.22mm
19swg	1.00mm
20swg	0.90mm
22swg	0.71mm
24swg	0.56mm
26swg	0.46mm
28swg	0.38mm
30swg	0.32mm
32swg	0.28mm
34swg	0.24mm
36swg	0.20mm

Stub wires come in lengths from 7" (18cm) to 20" (50cm) and are used to support, strengthen and control plant material.

wires can be moulded, threaded, crunched and bound into decorative designs for wedding work. Covered wires, such as paper- and hessian-covered wires, are used to bind, blend in, weave and tie together mediums that are a visible part of the design. Plastic-coated garden wires are stronger and heavier and are used for securing heavy mediums together.

Ribbon, Ties and Tape

Ribbon

A good selection of ribbons and ties is essential for most wedding work as these form an integral part of many designs. Use them to make bows and cover bouquet handles, incorporate them into bouquets as trails, use them to dress containers, tables and chairs and, most importantly, use them to tie stems together. There is a large variety of ribbons and other ties available from florist wholesalers, haberdasheries, and high street stores.

Polytie is a synthetic ribbon, which is strong, shiny, waterproof and handy not only at its whole width but when torn into smaller strips for tying, curling and making bows. Wired-edged ribbon will keep its shape when made into loops and bows, but the wired edges will rust and be spoiled if they come into contact with water, so store in a dry place. Satin ribbons can be used to bind the handles of bouquets, and are also good for adding trails and making soft bows. Organza ribbons can be made into soft bows and loops or just left hanging to catch the breeze. These ribbons are light and transparent. There are a variety of lace ribbons, made from cotton, man-made fabrics and elastic. Hessian, linen, cotton or tapestry-material ribbons can make bows, decorate jars and containers, and can be used as runners

Stub wires, reel wires, covered wires and decorative wires.

Ribbons, ties, cords and tapes.

on tablecloths. On the whole they are not waterproof.

Ties

Cords are strong, twisted materials used for tying, making bows and binding onto stems and containers for decoration. String can be a natural or a man-made material, and is available in various colours and thicknesses. String can be used for tying for security, binding onto stems for decorative purposes (buttonholes) and making into bows. It is practical, decorative and strong. Raffia is a strong natural fibre taken from the palm tree; it comes dyed in many colours or in its natural cream state and is used for tying, weaving, plaiting and finishing arrangements with rustic country-style bows and ties. If raffia becomes wet it will lose its form. It will dry out but some of its original shape will have been lost. Some dyed raffia may not be colourfast; check before tying to bride's bouquets, or just do not get it wet! Wool can be used to bind onto bouquet handles, drizzle over bouquets and tie onto buttonholes.

Tape

Pot tape is a specially manufactured adhesive tape. It comes in two widths in white or green, is strong, waterproof, and is used to secure floral foam into containers. It can be used to make a strong bond if wrapped around two mediums, and used to cover and protect exposed wirework. Double-sided tapes come in clear or white and are used to bond two mediums together. When applied, the tape is hidden between the two materials. Clear, waterproof, adhesive tape is used to secure floral foam into glass or transparent containers, or across containers to support stems. Clear tape can also be used to bind mediums together that require an unobtrusive fastening.

Sticky tape is for lighter use and is not watertight; it is usually mounted in heavy-base dispensers with a sharp cutting edge. The base will allow you one hand free to hold and stick paper, cellophane and tissue together. Stem-wrap tapes are for covering stems and wires. You can choose a waxy crêpe paper composite or a man-made plastic type, but both have an elastic characteristic useful for stretching and sealing. The paper type is available in different colours and is the cheapest of the stem-wrap types. Try both out and see which you prefer as bridal work consists of a large amount of taping.

Floral Foam

Floral foam is a water-retaining medium used to secure and hold stems of plant material into specific design shapes. There are many manufacturers of floral foam, each making their own densities and foams for various uses. Economy foam is for lightweight flowers, general-purpose foam is for standard arrangements and very dense foam is for larger arrangements to hold the heaviest stems. Dense foam also provides extra strength and grip right up to the edge. Sizes and shapes of foam vary from the smallest round posy cylinder, through

Floral foam.

general oblong blocks for cutting to size, to large designer shapes and wall tiles. To use floral foam, fill a large and deep container with water and float the floral foam, allowing the water to circulate freely and soak into the foam. Do not push or plunge the foam under the water as this allows air bubbles to get trapped, preventing the foam from soaking fully. The saturation time will vary from one manufacturer to another, but is usually ninety seconds or thereabouts. You will be able to see when the foam is soaked, as it will darken in colour slightly and sink so the top is just above the water's surface. Always use wet floral foam according to the manufacturer's instructions.

Spheres of floral foam are used for making pomanders, topiary trees and hanging designs. They are generally available in sizes from 3" (8cm) to 16" (41cm), and can be purchased already netted. Floral foam blocks (which come in various colours) have a dense composition and are both decorative and useful for giving firm support to plant material. Coloured foam can be used to keep wet arrangements in place and can be shaped and added to dry arrangements for additional interest. Wet foam rings are available in sizes from 8" (20cm) to 24" (60cm). Rings come either with a plastic base (these are suitable for table designs, as they won't leak water onto cloths) or a hard foam base (these can be used for outside decoration).

Bouquet Holders

Bouquet holders are plastics formed into a handle topped with a cage-type, foam-filled structure that is used to hold wet or dry floral foam. They come in various sizes and shapes, including round, square, oblong and heart-shaped, and with straight or angled handles. Wet floral foam bridal bouquet holders are

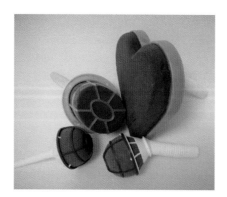

Bouquet holders.

useful for allowing you to arrange flowers that may be prone to wilting. Dry foam holders can be used for silk or fresh flowers that have a longer lasting capability.

Accessories

Alice bands come in different widths, and can be made from plastic, material-covered plastic or thin metal. Combs come in various sizes and are usually a lightweight clear plastic. Bracelets can be used as a base for making wrist corsages; there are many designs to choose from including plain, pearl, metal and beaded bracelets.

Sundries

- Watering cans with long spouts can be useful to reach and water the back of large arrangements.
- Spray mister with a fine spray setting is handy for misting finished floral designs with water.
- Spray paints are great for revitalizing recycled containers.
- A screwdriver and a hammer in your toolbox can come in handy for large structural designs that may need last-minute attention.
- Waterproof sheeting is useful for protecting surfaces as you work.
- Polybags are important for rubbish disposal.
- Flower food is essential for keeping plant material fresh, fed and alive for longer.
- Leaf shine can be used on leaves that are prominent in a design.
- Plain pins that can be hidden from view are good for securing fabrics and buttonholes.
- Pearl-headed and decorative pins can be used for buttonholes, corsages and as an integral part of the design.
- Sequins, beads and crystals are handy for adding that extra sparkle into a design.
- Safety pins are key for attaching garlands to tablecloths and pinning lightweight materials together.
- Magnets are used for attaching buttonholes and corsages to clothes.

Alice bands, combs and bracelets.

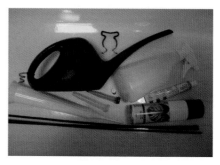

Sundries.

- Elastic bands are handy for joining together stems that require flexibility.
- Vials (plastic tubes with rubber caps that form a watertight seal around the stems pushed through them) can be covered in different mediums for concealment. Glass tubes without tops are also sometimes used. Both types of vial are used to hold and keep plant material fresh when wired into garlands and other designs that have no other means of retaining water.
- Canes come in many thicknesses and colours. 'Midelino' canes are thin but very flexible and can be used to build a cage surround for bridal bouquets or can be added into design pieces for a distinctive look. Garden canes are thicker and good for adding length to dried plant material and attaching to funnels to elevate and hold fresh flowers in large flower arrangements.
- Broom handle clips are good for attaching floral decorations to pew ends.
- Chicken wire can be used both in containers to support and position flowers and to make cages for floral foam garlands and arches.

Paper and Boxes

Various sizes of cardboard box are available for packing, delivering and

Wrapping paper, tissue paper and boxes.

presenting finished bridal work. These can be finished off with decorative wrapping paper. The colourfast tissue paper is used for packing, protecting and supporting flowers ready for delivery. Finally, cellophane can be used as a transparent waterproof film to cover and protect bridal flowers in their delivery boxes.

Containers

It is important to collect a variety of buckets and containers in different sizes for storing and supporting flowers with long and short stems. Pedestal stands, plinths, columns and milk churns can be used to display large, spectacular arrangements. Urns and vases can be used for floral displays on their own or mounted on pedestal stands for large arrangements.

Tip: Buy pedestal stands and large vases in matching pairs for standing either

side of the bride and groom, framing a doorway or on the chancel steps.

Also useful are plastic containers, such as round bowls for posies and large round bowls that will fit into the tops of pedestal stands, long trays for table runners and spray trays for pew ends and sprays. Rustic wooden crates can be used for stacking and as a base for large floral displays while smaller crates can be used on their own for meadow-box designs. Baskets in all shapes and sizes are handy for flower arrangements that have to be removed and reused or carried by young bridesmaids who will be throwing flowers or rose-petal confetti during the ceremony. Finally, glass jars, vintage teacups, tin cans, church candles, plastic containers and bottles can be used for small table posies.

Additional aids such as a first aid kit, apron and towels for spilt water are essential to have on hand.

Containers and pedestal stands.

Chapter 5

Looking After Flowers and Foliage

Whether you are buying commercially grown flowers and foliage, foraging in the countryside, or cutting from the garden, all plant material will benefit from some form of conditioning. Flowers purchased from wholesalers or florist shops should have already had the first stage of conditioning, but all stock will need further attention as soon as possible if the stems are left out of water for any length of time.

Conditioning

Conditioning is a term used to describe the preparation of flowers and foliage for decorative use. Good conditioning will help flowers look their best and last longer. The life of even the best-conditioned flowers will be shortened if they are placed near draughts and/or burning sunshine, yet these may be the very settings that show your floral display to best advantage.

All wedding flowers that are worn or carried have to be prepared only a short time before the ceremony to prevent wilting, but arrangements made in floral foam or vases of water for the church or venue can be done a day or two before the ceremony. Nevertheless it is a fine line between getting the flowers to full fruition for the best impact on the day, and them dying back or wilting.

Plants emit moisture through their pores through a process called transpiration, which is accelerated by heat and light. Moisture is removed more rapidly by dry air and draughts, and if plants cannot replace this quickly enough, flowers and plant material will dry out.

Once flowers are cut from a plant some continue to grow slowly and at the same time form a callous over the cut, meaning they have a diminished capability of receiving the nutrients that are vital for their survival (tulips can grow two centimetres a day). To give them all a head start, it is advisable to give them a good drink of water with the appropriate flower food added. As water is mostly taken up by absorption through the stems, this is where proper preparation starts.

Cutting the stems of plant material with a knife is preferable to using scissors. The cells in stems can be crushed when using scissors, restricting the absorption of water and damaging the plant, which can deprive the flower

Cutting stems away from the body at 45 degrees with a clean, sharp knife.

head of part or all of its supply. However, care must be taken when using very sharp knives, and it may be more practical to cut some stems with scissors due to their irregular shapes and angles. Heavier secateurs will be needed to cut stronger, woody stems.

Care

Spending a little extra time with your preparation will not only benefit the flowers but also prove more economical and less wasteful. All flowers need care when handling, especially wedding

LEFT: A jug of freshly picked garden flowers.

blooms that may have a delicate nature and fine stem structure, as with lily-of-the-valley (*Convallaria*). Flowers with white petals can be easily bruised if handled roughly, spoiling their starring role in the bride's bouquet.

Remove all wrappings from flower bunches as soon as possible and check and trim all damaged flowers and plant material before conditioning. Any wildlife found on flowers and leaves will need to be dispatched to avoid further damage. An uninvited guest on a table display or in the bride's bouquet may not receive a warm welcome!

Preparation

Bacteria can block the vascular system in the stems of plants and can be detrimental to their survival. Such bacteria grows easily in containers and buckets if they are not cleaned thoroughly. This may lead to a breakdown in plant tissue, smelly water and slimy stems. Scrub and wash out all receptacles with bleach to prevent bacteria forming and eliminate any contamination. Plastic buckets are light to handle and easy to clean; caution has to be taken when using metal containers as they may react to the use of flower food, which will affect the water and damage the flowers.

Flower Food

There are several types of flower food, which may come attached to the bunch, as with mimosa (*Acacia dealbata*) and lilac (*Syringa vulgaris*), which require special food that aids the flow of water up woody stems. Daffodils (*Narcissus*) and bulb flowers have a food that allows them to be mixed with other flowers. Roses, chrysanthemums (*Dendranthema*) and *Bouvardia* also have specific foods. All flower foods feed

the blooms with sugar, and have an anti-bacterial agent to prevent bacteria and an acidifier to balance the pH level in the water. These elements are, in fact, all the nourishment a plant needs to fulfil its maximum potential.

Fill buckets with cold but not freezing water and add the appropriate flower food for each type of flower according to the instructions on the packet. Use a universal type of flower food if no packet is presented with the bunch. Strip all foliage that will fall beneath the water line and, using a clean, sharp knife or scissors, cut at least 1" (2cm) off the stems at a 45-degree angle, then put in water straight away. Cut and defoliate all flower and foliage stems in this way before conditioning. This will give the flowers a larger area with which to absorb water; flat-cut stems may sit on the bottom of the bucket and be less able to take up water.

Additional Conditioning

Flowers with large heads, such as lilies, take up a lot of water, so you may have to top up throughout the conditioning period. To prevent staining from pollen found on stamens inside the lily flower, pick it out right away. If any pollen falls onto cloths, remove with sticky tape; do not try to rub it off as this usually rubs the pollen in.

Lily showing stamens.

Removing stamens from inside lily flowers.

Chrysanthemums, daffodils and hippeastrums can be purchased from wholesalers dry-packed and will recover readily when rehydrated, but it will take a day or two for the larger blooms to open. Roses are bunched with their heads packed tightly together and should be unpacked and separated as soon as possible to avoid damp patches browning the petals.

Transvaal daisies (*Gerbera*) should be conditioned with their heads supported and their stems left to dangle free; this will keep their stems straight. For these flowers, 2" (5cm) of water is sufficient. Too much water may cause them to drown because there are no leaves to nourish and the water goes straight to the flower head.

Flowers that exude latex fluid from their stems, for example poppies (*Papaver*), and anything from the spurge (*Euphorbia*) family, can be singed by holding the cut end in a flame (gas or candle) for a few seconds until black. Follow this by putting the stems into water. Daffodils release a sap, which can be poisonous to other flowers, so condition this group of flowers separately unless using specific flower food.

To keep tulips straight, they should be wrapped firmly in paper before cutting the stems and putting in water. Sometimes this doesn't stop tulips seeking out the light (tropism), so

Bucket with wire mesh topping, supporting gerbera heads.

undulating, curvaceous stems may not be avoided.

Hollow stems of large delphinium and hippeastrum can be upturned and filled with water, using a narrow-spouted watering can. Plug the ends with cotton wool, which will act as a wick, before placing in water.

Wilted flowers such as hydrangea, lilac, and roses can be revived by submerging completely in water and leaving for a few hours. Wilted roses can also be treated by plunging the tip of the stem into boiling water for about thirty seconds, then into tepid water for conditioning. Protect the rose's bloom by holding away from the heat. Do not remove thorns at this stage, as the open scar is susceptible to infection.

Hard, woody stems should have about 2" (5cm) of bark scraped off in addition to having their stems cut before putting in water. This exposes a greater area of the inside of the stem for better water absorption.

Carnations (*Dianthus caryophyllus*) should be cut between the nodes on the stem. The nodes, when cut into, do not have the capability to take up water.

If mimosa is purchased with a polythene bag covering the flower heads, this should be left on while conditioning. Otherwise, a regular misting will keep the flowers from drying out.

Orchid (*Dendrobium* and *Cymbidium*) stems need to be removed from their vials, recut at 45 degrees and put in fresh water with flower food. Stems that are heavily loaded with flower heads will need supporting.

Storing

Cut flowers and foliage, for example, tulips, roses, carnations, chrysanthemums, daffodils, lilies (including the Peruvian lily aka

Alstroemeria), anemones and freesias, can be stored at between 5–9°C. This will be cold enough to keep the flowers in good condition, but will also allow blooms to come to fruition. Leave all flowers and foliage to drink for at least two hours or ideally overnight before using. If no cold store or refrigeration unit is available, place flowers in a cool, draught-free but well-ventilated place, away from direct sunlight. Tropical flowers such as the painter's palette (*Anthurium*), glory lily (*Gloriosa*), hanging lobster claw (*Heliconia*) or Amazon lily (*Eucharis*) need to be stored in a warmer place at 16°C.

Cutting Flowers from the Garden or Foraging in the Countryside

Cutting in the early morning or at the end of the day will produce stronger flowers than cutting at midday when they have lost a great deal of moisture to the heat of the sun. Take a container of water with you and place the stems in it as soon as you cut them. If this is not practical, take some plastic bags with you, put the flowers in and seal the bag to keep the moisture in. You will need to recut the stems for final conditioning. When flowers and foliage are left out of water for even a short time after cutting, the tips of the stems may dry out and become less able to absorb water. Air bubbles may also form and block the uptake of water. Evergreen foliage may have to be washed if dirty or dusty. Tepid water with a small amount of washing-up liquid can be used, then rinse with clean water.

Although many types of foliage and flowers can to be purchased from wholesalers, there are some shrubs, trees, annual and perennial flowers that can be successfully grown in the garden. Easy access to some plant material will not only be convenient, but also economical and timesaving. Of course, suitable soil types and positioning in the garden will vary and should you wish to go down this route further research will be needed.

The foliage cut from trees and shrubs mentioned here is the most frequently used for floristry, and is reasonably fast-growing and easy to cultivate. It can be cut throughout the year, minimizing the need for pruning. Cut only what is needed for each arrangement each time, leaving the rest for another day! If a few flower heads are left on lady's mantle (*Alchemilla mollis*), love-in-a-mist (*Nigella damascena*), poppies and loosestrife, they will self-seed and reward you with additional flowering plants for the following year.

Griselinia littoralis

This shrub has fresh, limey green leaves (sometimes with a cream/white edge). It grows best in a light position. The long stems that it produces can be used for large and medium arrangements. It is evergreen and lasts very well in floral foam. For a symmetrical arrangement, cut stems from the right side of the bush for the right side of the arrangement, and the left side of the bush for the left side. This will give the best shape of stem for each side without too much snipping and adjusting. This foliage can be used for hand-tied designs and posies.

Foliage, from left to right: griselinia, variegated pittosporum, green pittosporum, euonymus, and ivy.

Pittosporum tenuifolium

This evergreen tree has woody stems and dense, small, wavy leaves, which are either shiny green or grey/white and green. It will tolerate regular cutting and lasts very well in floral foam. Use it for hand-tied bouquets, arrangements and as filler foliage.

Euonymus fortunei (Spindle Tree)

This evergreen shrub has short-branched stems and hardy, long-lasting leaves.

Varieties can have plain, shiny, green leaves, or leaves with additional yellow markings. Spindle tree is used in traditional arrangements, hand-tied bouquets, buttonholes, corsages and circlets, and is also good for basing, groundwork or as a filler foliage. Wipe clean individual leaves used for wirework, and store on dampened kitchen paper in a cool, dark place to keep fresh.

Hedera helix (Ivy)

This popular English foliage can be grown in shade or sun and left to climb up a wall or fence. It has the benefit of three forms for use in floristry. When the ivy reaches the top of its given support, it will then produce long trails. The long trailing stems can be used in bouquets, cascading in pedestals, and making collars in hand-tied designs. If left at the top of its growth, it will reach the 'arborescent' stage, which is dense and woody. Flowers will develop at this

Foliage, from left to right: rosemary, panicum, myrtle, Senecio maritima, brachyglottis, and eucalyptus.

point, followed by balls of black berries. This compact growth along with the berries can be useful for giving texture to hand-tied designs and floral arrangements. Individual leaves can be cut for buttonholes and wirework. There are many varieties of ivy, from plants with small, pointed leaves to those with large and glossy leaves. Colours range from dark green to yellow, and some leaves have cream-marbled centres or edges. Individual leaves used for wiring and wearing on apparel or the body should be wiped clean and stored in the cool, on damp kitchen towel until needed. Although this plant is an evergreen and much loved for winter wedding work, the new growth in spring will not be turgid enough to use.

Rosmarinus officinalis (Rosemary)

This bushy, evergreen herb is aromatic and fragrant and produces small, blue flowers in early summer. Grown in a sunny position it will produce the best stalks and flowers. Use in hand-tied bouquets, small posies, table arrangements and buttonholes.

Panicum virgatum, Pennisetum (Grasses)

As a general rule, pick the flower-producing stems just before the seed head has busted out of its sheaf. If harvested too late in its development it may well cause a problem with the uncontrolled scattering of seeds, spoiling any material it comes into contact with. Handle the stems with care, as they tend to bend easily. Use in hand-tied designs and arrangements.

Myrtus communis (Myrtle)

This dark green shrub produces long, woody stems with small leaves. It will survive in full sun or semi-shade. The

small, fluffy, white flowers that cover the bush in August have the most delightful perfume. Little black berries follow the flowers and are useful for textural designs. Even the leaves are aromatic when handled, so it's no wonder this shrub is used for bridal bouquets and headdresses. Larger stems can be used for outline foliage in pedestal arrangements; smaller pieces look dainty in posies.

Senecio maritima

Although this plant is used for summer bedding, it survives well through the winter and lasts in the garden for a number of years, if planted in full sun. Its silver-grey, deeply cut leaves are very attractive and lacy-looking. It is good for using in vintage-style bridal bouquets, and wirework, both for summer and winter weddings, and can also be used in floral foam, where it is long-lasting. Avoid getting the leaves wet, as their furry surface will be damaged.

Brachyglottis (Daisy Bush, also Known as Senecio 'Sunshine')

This is a very easy to grow, medium-sized evergreen shrub, with grey-green leaves on woody stems. Plant it in full sun. The short stems are good for hand-tied bouquets, small posies and in buttonholes, corsages and headdresses. Avoid getting the leaves wet, as this will spoil the soft grey texture on the underside of the leaves.

Eucalyptus cinerea (Gum Tree)

This tree will quickly get out of hand without regular cutting; it likes to be planted in a sunny spot, but will survive in semi-shade. Its long, woody, gracious stems with grey-green leaves are aromatic and long-lasting, and can be used in hand-tied designs, buttonholes, corsages and floral foam arrangements.

Alchemilla mollis (Lady's Mantle)

This delightful perennial has only a small flower but it is such a brilliant lime green that it shows up well and also seems to enhance other colours. It can be used in hand-tied bouquets, posies, wirework and lasts very well in floral foam. The round leaves are also attractive when used to cover mechanics. If the stems are cut just before all the flowers are open, they will continue to develop in the following days during conditioning. You may also get a second flowering later in the year. This plant prefers a light position in the garden but will also grow in semi-shade.

Lonicera (Honeysuckle)

This sweet-smelling English garden climber is not very long-lasting in hand-tied bouquets, and will last a few days in floral foam but its attractive form creates texture and variety. It is not commercially produced. To get the maximum rewards from this flower, cut just as the buds are beginning to open and let them fully blossom when assembled into a design or bouquet.

Dianthus barbatus (Sweet William)

A biennial plant grown by seed or cuttings, it likes a sunny position. The compact flower heads are white, pink, red or deep burgundy and have a mild perfume. It is excellent for bulking up hand-tied designs and will last well in floral foam for table posies. Cut when the flower head is fully formed between the nodes.

Tanacetum parthenium (Feverfew)

A herb with citrus-scented leaves and dainty, daisy-like white flowers with a yellow centre. This plant likes a sunny position and will spread around the

Flowers, from left to right: lady's mantle, honeysuckle, Sweet William feverfew, poppies: open, seed head and in bud, loosestrife, love-in-a-mist: seed head and flower.

garden over several seasons. Use for summer country weddings in hand-tied bouquets, but note that it does not last long out of water. It will last in floral foam for posies if you are careful with the thin, delicate stems.

Papaver (Poppy)

This plant's pink, purple and white blousy flowers borne on long stems are only usable if picked when the flower bud is just showing colour, but not fully open. Although short-lived they do well in floral foam or in hand-tied bouquets if assembled at the very last moment before delivery. If left to develop seed heads, they become a very attractive misty blue/grey colour. They are long-lasting and can be used for wirework or dried for winter arrangements. Use the 'singe' method of conditioning for the flowers. No conditioning is necessary for the seed heads; they will dry out on their own and can be stored in a warm, dark, airy place.

Lythrum salicaria (Loosestrife)

This is a plant with purple or pink slender flower spikes that can grow and set seed freely around the garden with no special attention. It can tolerate shade or a sunny position. It lasts very well in arrangements in water or floral foam, but will not stay turgid enough for use in hand-tied bouquets.

Nigella damascena (Love-in-a-Mist)

An annual plant with delicate blue or white flowers followed by bulbous, misty-looking seed heads. Each stem carries both flower and seed head at the same time. As they flower from June to September these plants look pretty when included in country-style hand-ties or table posies and jam jars. The stems are very thin so handle with care.

Poisonous Flowers and Plants

When cutting and stripping leaves from stems ready for conditioning, you should be aware of the potential risk of poisoning from certain flowers and plants. Wearing rubber gloves and regularly washing hands will offer protection. Brides carrying hand-tied bouquets for several hours may be at risk of harm, as stems in these are largely left unprotected and exposed to the skin. Therefore it is advisable to avoid known poisonous varieties in bouquets. Berries should be kept of out reach of small children who sometimes mistake them for sweets.

Stored flowers and foliage in buckets and containers.

POISONOUS FLOWERS AND PLANTS

Aconitum (monkshood) – all parts poisonous

Aesculus hippocastanum (horse chestnut) – all parts poisonous

Agrostemma githago (corn cockle) – seeds poisonous

Alstroemeria (Peruvian lily) – may cause skin allergy

Arum maculatum (Lords and Ladies/cuckoo pint) – all parts poisonous

Aucuba japonica (spotted laurel) – all parts poisonous

Caladium (angel's Wings/elephant ears) – sap can be an irritant

Chrysanthemum – leaves can be an irritant

Clematis vitalba (old man's beard) – all parts poisonous and sap an irritant

Codiaeum (croton/Joseph's coat) – can be an irritant

Colchium – all parts poisonous

Convallaria majalis (lily-of-the-valley) – all parts poisonous

Cupressocyparis leylandii – may cause skin allergy

Daphne mezereum – all parts poisonous and an irritant

Dicentra spectabilis (bleeding heart) – all parts poisonous

Dieffenbachia (leopard lily/dumb cane) – all parts poisonous and an irritant

Digitalis (foxglove) – all parts poisonous

Euonymus europaeus (spindle) - all parts poisonous

Euphorbia (all hard species/spurge) – all parts poisonous, sap an irritant

Euphorbia milii (crown of thorns) – all parts poisonous, sap an irritant

Fraxinus excelsior (ash) – all parts poisonous, sap an irritant

Galanthus nivalis (snowdrop) – all parts poisonous

Gloriosa superba (glory lily) – all parts poisonous

Hedera helix (ivy) – all parts poisonous and an irritant

Helleborus (Christmas rose) – all parts poisonous and an irritant

Hippeastrum (amarylis) – all parts poisonous

Hyacinthus (hyacinth) – all parts poisonous, bulb an irritant

Hyacinthus non scriptus (bluebell) – all parts poisonous, bulb an irritant

Ilex aquifolium (holly) – berries poisonous

Ipomoea purpurea (morning glory) – all parts poisonous

Kalmia latifolia (calico bush) – all parts poisonous

Laburnum – all parts poisonous, especially bark and seeds

Lantana camara – all parts poisonous

Lathyrus odoratus (sweetpea) – seeds are poisonous

Ligustrum (privet) – all parts poisonous and an irritant

Lonicera (honeysuckle) – an irritant

Monstera deliciosa (Swiss cheese plant) – all parts poisonous and an irritant

Narcissus (daffodil) – all parts poisonous and sap an irritant

Nerium oleander – all parts poisonous

Ornithogalum umbellatum (star of Bethlehem) – all parts poisonous and an irritant

Papaver somniferum (opium poppy) – all parts poisonous

Philodendron (sweetheart vine) – an irritant

Physalis alkekengi (Chinese lantern) – unripe berry poisonous

Primula obconica (poison primula) – an irritant

Prunus laurocerasus (cherry laurel) – all parts poisonous

Rheum rhaponticum (rhubarb) – leaves poisonous

Ricinus communis (castor oil plant) – all parts poisonous, especially seeds

Ruta graveolens (rue) – an irritant

Sambucus nigra (elder) – all parts poisonous

Scindapsus aureus (Devil's ivy) – an irritant

Sedum acre (biting stonecrop) – an irritant

Solanum capsicastrum (winter cherry) – all parts poisonous

Symphoricarpos albus (snowberry) – all parts poisonous

Taxus baccata (yew) – seeds and leaves poisonous

Thuja occidentalis (white cedar) – all parts poisonous and an irritant

Tulipa (tulip) – all parts poisonous and an irritant

Veratrum nigrum (black false hellebore) – all parts poisonous

Chapter 6

Techniques

Wires have long been a part of floristry in one form or another and are an essential medium for wedding work. Today we have an enormous range of wires, allowing the development and flexibility of many creative design ideas and styles. All wirework must be carried out at the last possible moment before the wedding, as some flowers will only last a few hours before wilting. The weather, the distance for delivery and storing conditions are all contributory factors, along with the choice of flower. There may be several different technical methods of supporting each flower and foliage element, but as long as the method chosen successfully achieves the following it has done its job. The easiest way to remember which wires to use is: the thickest are for heavy stems and the thinnest are used for lighter stems.

The purpose of wire
- To strengthen and support stems of foliage and flowers.
- To control plant material so it can be used in any position.
- To reduce weight (by removing the stem and replacing with wire).
- To keep flowers and foliage in an anchored position.

- For use as a false stem to lengthen a piece of material.
- For binding bouquets and plant material together.
- To make a framework for mounting flowers.
- To add distinctive decorative elements to designs.

Use of Wire

Use the lightest wire possible to support and strengthen the corresponding plant material whilst retaining some movement and flexibility. When possible, conceal wire internally. To prevent the finished assembly becoming heavy, do not over-wire. Wires should be as unobtrusive as possible.

External Wiring

Insert the wire into the base of the calyx (seed box) or head of the flower and wind down. External wiring is generally used for thicker stems.

Internal Wiring

Insert the wire completely within the stem of the flower; this is particularly useful on soft or hollow stems.

External wiring of gerbera.

Hook Wiring

Small flowers and daisies can be wired by inserting the wire up into the stem and out of the top of the flower head,

Hook wiring of daisy chrysanthemum.

Single-leg mount of fern.

Gypsophila – natural bunch wired.

Wire hook pulled through to top of flower.

Double-leg mount of myrtle.

Cross wiring, lisy.

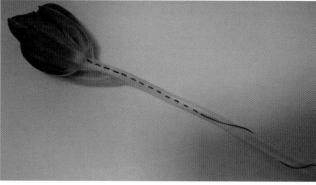

Wire pushed internally into the top 4″ (10cm) of the tulip stem to reach the flower head, and winding externally down the lower part.

bending the wire over into a hairpin shape and gently pulling the wire down again until the hairpin makes contact with the centre of the bloom.

Semi-Internal Wiring

Insert the wire internally into the stem at the top of the flower a short distance

from and into the calyx, and then bring the wire down externally, winding it around the lower part of the stem.

Mount Wiring

This is used to control or lengthen a stem in bridal bouquets, headdresses, corsages and buttonholes.

A single-leg mount is used for lighter-weight plant material, creating a false stem for wired wedding work.
A double-leg mount is used for slightly heavier plant material, and is also used for wired wedding work.

Natural bunched stems can be wired either with single-leg mount for light stems, or a double-leg mount for heavier stems.

Cross Wiring

Cross wiring can also be used to keep flower heads from snapping off their stems. Push one wire horizontally into and across the calyx and insert another wire up into the stem vertically. Bring the

Cross wiring, lisy.

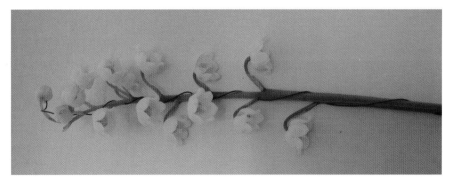

Wiring lily-of-the-valley.

cross wire down to meet the vertical wire and wind around. Choose wires suitable to the weight of the flower head.

Pinning in Vines, Trailing Moss and Streamers

For attaching trails of plant material and streamers to finished designs, cut and bend a suitable gauge wire into a hairpin. Snag the trail or streamer into the hairpin with a twist and push the hairpin firmly and securely into the foam.

Pinning in trails of moss.

Wiring Lily-of-the-valley

Starting at the bottom of the stem, wind the wire up and around the little flower heads until you reach the top. The stems are very fine and delicate so take extra care. Finish and cut the wire close to the base of the last floret and tuck the wire in. To keep the wiring as unobtrusive as possible, use a green 36swg (0.20mm) reel wire.

Traditional Buttonholes

Buttonholes have evolved from medieval times when a knight would wear a lady's colours tied either to his wrist or to the reins of his horse. This later transferred to men wearing favours in a hatband and, with the introduction of the formal suit, into the top pocket or a ready-made hole in the lapel. Typically, a single flower is used with or without added foliage. Napoleon Bonaparte's most avid admirers would use a red carnation tucked deep into the top pocket of their suit to simulate the *Legion d'Honneur* medal.

Attaching a Buttonhole

To attach a buttonhole, insert the wired stem down into the hole as far as it will go, turn the lapel forward and pin the buttonhole into the back of the material diagonally across, catching the stem of the flower and making sure the pin does not come through to the front of the lapel and stick out. Replace the lapel and adjust the leaves to sit comfortably against the material. Buttonholes are always pinned on the left side for both men and women. It's where the heart is! For grooms or other guests in the armed services, permission will be required to pin a wedding favour to their military uniform where medals are attached.

Tip: Many new suits are manufactured with their buttonholes stitched closed. When delivering to the groom, take a pair of small, sharp scissors with you and offer to cut it open and pin the flower in if necessary.

Rose Buttonhole

MATERIALS
3 ivy leaves
1 rose
Wires: 3 x 30swg (0.32mm) wires for the leaves and 1 x 22swg
(0.71mm) wire for the rose
Stem wrap
Flower scissors capable of cutting low gauge wires

METHOD
Wipe the leaves clean and cut the stems to 1″ (3cm) length.
Stitch each leaf by inserting a 30swg (0.32mm) wire diagonally
across the centre vein about three quarters of the way up.

Using your thumb and finger to hold the wire in place will
prevent the leaf from tearing. Bend down the two sides of the
wire until they are parallel to the stem.

Take one wire and wind it around the other wire and
shortened stem several times, ending with the two wires
parallel again, one wire short and one long.

Rose buttonhole.

Back of ivy leaf wired diagonally across
the vein.

Thumb and finger holding wire over ivy
leaf.

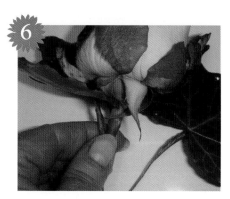

Bending wires down to horizontal
position.

Taping ivy leaf.

Rose with two wires inserted into its stem

Adding ivy leaves to wired rose.

Tape

The purpose of tape
- To conceal wires
- To seal in and retain moisture within the stem
- To protect the wearer's clothes from damage

How to Apply Stem-wrap Tape

Hold one end of the tape firmly against and at a slight angle across the top of the stem or wire with the thumb and forefinger of one hand, then pull the tape gently to create tension with the other hand. You will see the tape stretching. Keeping the tension, guide the tape diagonally down the stem, while at the same time twisting the stem with the other hand. One hand stays twisting, while the other hand continues to guide the tape. Break the tape off when you reach the end of the stem. The warmth of your hands will make the tape easier to stretch. Next, wire and tape the two remaining leaves.

Check for and discard any damaged petals and cut the stem of the rose approximately $1^1/_2$" (4cm). Insert two 22swg (0.71mm) wires up into the stem, piercing the calyx, one at a time, then cut the wires to a length of approximately 3" (8cm). (If only one wire is used, it sometimes swivels around when applying stem wrap.) Apply the stem wrap as above.

Place the three leaves evenly around the stem of the rose, with the largest at the back and one either side. Tape them all together. Cut the stem to the correct length and add a pin, then box, mist with water, cover with cellophane, label and keep cool until required.

Ribbon

Making a Bow

METHOD
Make a figure of eight with as many loops as you like (the more loops there are, the fuller the bow will be). The loops will determine the finished width of the bow. More control of the ribbon is gained by making the bow in the hand.

Holding the ribbon at the crossover point, loop the ribbon back over onto itself, making a figure-of-eight. Loop back over to the first loop, and continue looping back and forth until the desired

Ribbon bow.

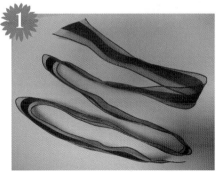

Make loops in figure-of-eight.

Pinch loops together.

Tie loops at the pinch point.

A raffia bow with wire and stem wrap.

fullness is reached, then pinch and hold the central crossover point before cutting the end.

With an extra length of ribbon, tie the loops all together in the centre at the crossover point.

Straighten out the loops of the finished bow.

WIRED BOW
Follow the instructions for making a bow, but use 36swg (0.20mm) of silver wire at the central crossover point to secure the loops, twist the wire and cover with stem wrap. This type of bow is suitable for including in wirework for wedding bouquets, headdresses and corsages.

Corsages

A corsage is a small group of flowers and/or foliage fashioned into a shape for personal adornment to suit the wearer. Styles can be decorative, wired or glued but should be kept as lightweight as possible. Care must be taken to protect clothes from open wires, unless they are the decorative type and part of the design. Corsages can be attached to clothing with a pin, a magnet or a ready-made corsage attachment. Wearing the corsage on the left-hand side will ensure it does not get in the way of a romantic first waltz where you can rest your head on the shoulder of your partner!

Traditionally the groom, as a token of affection, presents a corsage to the mother of the bride as part of the wedding rituals. These corsage designs can be made to fit on a lapel, wrist, hat or handbag.

Tip: Always ask the weight of fabric a corsage is to be attached to. Some fine silks and delicate materials may not be suitable for a corsage, which could cause dragging; in these situations, a handbag spray may be more suitable.

Corsage

MATERIALS
1 sprig of lavender foliage
4 small sprigs of eucalyptus foliage
3 senecio leaves
4 lamb's ears
6 French lavender flower heads
3 small roses
Wires
Stem wrap

A simple rose corsage.

Beginning to assemble the corsage.

Prepared flowers and leaves for a corsage.

Adding more flowers.

Adding flowers either side.

Raffia bow
Pearl-headed pin

METHOD
Check for any damage to flowers and
leaves and discard if necessary. Starting
with a leaf, introduce a flower on one
side of the leaf and tape, then another
on the other side and tape. Continue
adding flowers and leaves either side
one at a time travelling a little further
down and taping each one in place as
you go. Add the first rose in the middle
and tape in place.

Continue adding more flowers and
leaves, travelling as you go.

Continue adding further flowers and
leaves, travelling and taping each flower
until you reach the desired length, then
bend the final few leaves and flowers
over the stem to face down and tape in
place. Add the bow and tape in place,
cut the wires to about a third of the
length of the completed design and tape
to secure.

Finish the design by adjusting the last
leaves over the front of the stem. Add a
pearl-headed pin into the stem. Finally,
box, mist with water, cover with
cellophane, label and keep cool until
required.

Country Posy Corsage

A country posy corsage contrives to look
like a natural grouping of flowers and
plant material, but is wired, taped and
manipulated into a desired shape.

METHOD
Gather a selection of wired and taped
small country-garden flowers including
sweet William, poppy-seed head, love-in-
the-mist flower and seed head, feverfew
and lady's-mantle.

Arrange the flowers in your hand into
a posy. At this stage you can adjust the
positioning until a pleasing natural
shape is formed.

A country-bunch corsage.

Prepared flowers for a country corsage.

Grouping flowers together.

Gluing ribbon.

Gather all the stems together two-
thirds of the way down the bunch, and
glue ribbon around the stems to secure
them. Separate and cut the stems to
length.

Once you have the finished design
with stems splayed out to look like a
natural bunch, add a pearl-headed pin.
Finally, box, mist with water, cover with
cellophane and keep cool until
required.

Cold gluing has its advantages for incorporating dried and fresh plant materials and beads into designs very fast, and is useful for repairing and disguising last-minute damage. It is easy to use, saves time and creates lightweight designs, often eliminating wiring and taping. The disadvantage is that flowers and foliage are quite often glued into a flat position, and once joined there is no second chance or flexibility to reposition the plant material.

Applying Glue

Before you start, make sure the two sides of the medium to be joined are dry, at room temperature and clean. Condensation will not allow the glue to set securely. Apply glue to both pieces of the medium you want to join, wait a few seconds until tacky and then press together to bond. Make sure the glue covers all cut areas of plant material to seal in and retain any moisture. Glue will not dry properly if the arrangement is refrigerated before the glue sets. Cold glue dries clear, is waterproof and won't damage fresh plant material.

Tip: Glue can be removed from sticky fingers with nail-varnish remover.

The Rustic Bunch (Boutonnière)

A rustic bunch or boutonnière is attached to the outside of the wearer's clothes with a pin or magnet. The finished stems in this arrangement are bulky and therefore not suitable for inserting into a cut buttonhole on a jacket or suit, or pinning to lightweight dress material. Woody stems that do not seep sap and dried plant materials can be used without wiring and taping, but flowers that leak, or need to retain moisture to stay fresh and keep from staining clothes, will need to be wired then sealed with stem wrap.

A rustic bunch buttonhole.

METHOD
Select a few small flowers and/or foliage and wire and tape the leaky and vulnerable flowers as required. Add in the dry-stem flowers and tie with string, decorative ribbon or raffia. Cut the stems to size and add a pin to the finished stems. Finally, box, mist with water, cover with cellophane and keep cool until required.

Tip: When fresh stems are used unwired and untaped they dehydrate and shrink and are prone to dropping out of the buttonhole. Be sure to tie them securely to avoid this.

For rosemary with new growth or which is in flower, I would recommend taping, otherwise a small mature sprig may stand on its own.

Pocket Posy

Pocket posies are a decorative strip of flowers glued onto card and either attached with magnets to a false pocket-top, or inserted via a length of card with flowers mounted on a top flap into the top pocket of a jacket. For this style of buttonhole you can use any bits and bobs that will last out of water.

MATERIALS
Pinch of 'grandfather's whiskers'
(Caustis recurvata)
5 very small lavender flowers
1 flower head of spray aster
3 house-leek heads
1 large aucuba leaf

Tape measure
Card
Cold glue
Knife
Flower scissors
2 magnets for method 2

METHOD 1
Measure across the top pocket. Measure, mark out and cut the card to size following the dotted line so it will fit into the depth of the pocket with extra for the flap over the top, orange scissors. With the yellow knife score into the card

A pocket posy.

along the continuous line, but do not sever completely.

Wipe the leaf clean, place onto the flap and glue into position.

Very carefully cut around the edge of the glued leaf.

Work out a pattern or position for the plant material before gluing. When you are happy with the design start gluing one piece at a time, until the pocket posy is complete.

Make sure all the glue is dry and cleaned away from the card before bending over the flap and inserting into the pocket.

Materials for a pocket posy.

Measuring the pocket.

The knife shows where to score the card, and the scissors where to cut the card.

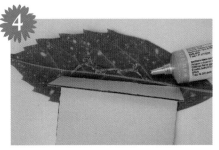

Cut the leaf to the size of the flap.

Cut out a section of leaf.

Gluing the flowers.

Inserting the finished posy into the pocket.

METHOD 2

Method 2 is for use on false pocket tops and is secured with magnets.

Cut out a piece of card to match the shape and size of the false pocket-top. Glue flowers and foliage onto the card all as before and glue two magnets onto the back of the card. Now, box, mist with water, cover with cellophane, and keep cool until required.

Tip: Recipients may be unsure of how to attach either of these two designs, so giving them a helping hand will be appreciated. Or you might demonstrate how to apply the posy to the pocket.

Handbag Spray

Handbag sprays are corsage-style assemblies of flowers, foliage and other decorative accessories. Design and size will depend on the style, colour and size of the handbag, which will have to be viewed in advance of the wedding so you can determine the method of fixing. The method of attachment will vary, but must be unobtrusive and practical so as to allow the handbag to be opened and not be damaged in any way.

MATERIALS
6 small roses
13 small pieces of Cineraria maritima
3 eucalyptus nuts
3 silver brunia heads
8 English lavender stalks

1 length of gauge wire that will fit around and over the flap of the bag that will hold the corsage
1 x 20swg (0.90mm) 19" (500mm) long green-coated wire is used here
Pot tape

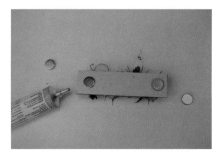

Gluing magnets to back of card.

A handbag corsage.

The finished pocket posy.

Prepared flowers and materials for the corsage.

Select small, suitable flowers and foliage and wire and tape as required.

Use pot tape to hide and secure the wire in place. Always ask permission to use tapes as they may leave a sticky residue when removed.

METHOD

Leave a length of wire to bend back over the inside flap, making sure the two ends connect with extra for joining them together. Start adding flowers and foliage, travelling along the wire. A diagonal design allows space for carrying.

Continue to add flowers and foliage as in all previous corsage instructions until you reach two-thirds of the length of the wire, then trim surplus wires.

Make a second, smaller corsage with a bow (at a third of the finished length), independent of the long wire, to match the first corsage.

Tape the second corsage onto the long wire in the opposite direction to join into the first corsage, butting them closely together. Adjust the flowers and leaves over any gaps to complete and finish the design. It should now look seamless.

While carefully supporting the flowers on the outside of the handbag, bring the wires diagonally across the inside of the handbag flap and twist together to secure. Squeeze the wire over both ends of the flap to pinch the fabric, creating a firmer grip.

Use pot tape to cover the diagonal wire. Do not mist with water as this may cause damage to the handbag surface. Just box, cover with cellophane and keep cool until needed.

Bend wire to fit shape, adding flowers.

Trimming wires.

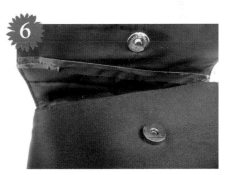
Make another smaller corsage.

Bending the stem and taping it into position.

Squeeze wires over each end of the handbag.

Cover the wire with tape.

Headddresses

Brides and bridesmaids have worn headdresses, in particular circlets of flowers, since Roman times. These were made by recognized florists of the time. The inner bark of the lime tree (bast) was used to plait or weave flowers into rings. The word 'wreath' is derived from the Greek for plaiting or twisting, and 'crown' is from the Latin for anything curved. In medieval Britain the Druids are often depicted wearing circlets of flowers. Although this predates the Roman period, there appears to be no written evidence of their construction or purpose. The headdresses were used in rites and rituals but we cannot be certain they were used for marriage ceremonies. However, the unbroken circlet is a symbol of maidenhood!

Flowers worn on the head must complement the volume of hair, style of hair and overall stature of the bride or bridesmaids. Attention to detail is all-important, as any flowers worn on the head will be seen all around and at eye level. All trimming must be neatly managed and wires concealed, avoiding any discomfort or snagging of the veil. To be worn comfortably and confidently, any style of headdress must be evenly balanced and provisions made for secure fixing.

Alice Band Headdress

Alice band headdresses can be made on a plastic or metal manufactured frame or on an independent framework of wires. Alice bands fit over the top of the head, from ear to ear. Measuring young bridesmaids heads before you make their headdresses will stop fidgeting caused by an overlap of flowers tickling behind their little ears. It is also beneficial to try on the manufactured bands as the compression points either side of the head may be too tight and cause discomfort.

Flowers mounted onto manufacturer's Alice band.

MATERIALS
10 medium roses
28 leaves, senecio and lamb's ear.
Alice band (this one has a cotton covering)
30swg (0.32mm) stub wires
Stem wrap

METHOD
Wire and tape all flowers and foliage. The lamb's ear leaves are bent in half, wired and taped into a looped position.

Firstly, measure the length needed to fit the dimensions of the Alice band before you start, and mark the middle. Starting with the soft 'lamb's ears' foliage, make two matching corsages of equal size.

Lay the corsages side by side, parallel to each other, to check they are a

matching pair.

Using the 30swg (0.32mm) wires, join the two corsages together by looping the wire over both stems and twisting, using one in the middle and two further wires either side. Bring the wires down vertically from the flowers.

Match the centre wire of the completed corsages with the centre of the Alice band and, using the same wires, attach the flowers to the Alice band, joining all the wires one by one. Make sure the ends of the wires are tucked in to avoid snagging the hair.

With the stem wrap, neatly tape over all five wires. Adjust the flowers over the central area to close any gaps, then box, mist with water, cover with cellophane, and keep cool until needed.

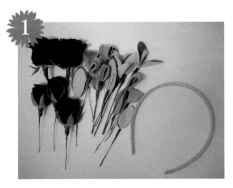

Prepared flowers and foliage.

Two corsages made the same size.

Laying the two corsages parallel.

Join the two corsages together with five equally placed wires.

Wire onto the Alice band.

Tape over the wires to avoid any sharp ends.

Comb

A variety of combs can be purchased from florist wholesalers, or ask for one to be provided if the wearer has a preference. Combs decorated with fresh flowers can be delicate, so careful handling is necessary when attaching to the head. Such combs are not intended to be the mainstay for holding hairstyles in place, but as a secondary means of decoration. However, combs can be used at the top of the head at the point where a veil is attached, on the side of the head or at the back of the head into a chignon hairstyle.

MATERIALS
3 small roses
3 small pieces of cockscomb
3 sea holly
5 small sprigs of sea lavender
4 heads of brunia
4 eucalyptus nuts
4 triteleia
Comb

Wires
Stem wrap
Tape
Seashells threaded onto bullion wire

A comb for a seaside wedding.

Prepared flowers, seashells and comb.

METHOD

Wire and tape all the flowers, and make into two small corsages to fit the size of the comb. Follow the instructions for corsages, or for the Alice band, as the method of assembly is the same for the comb.

An alternative piece can be made without the comb, by mounting the flowers on a wire with two loops at either end for attaching hairgrips to the head.

Join the two corsages together by wiring the stems in the middle and one each side. This shows the 'stay-wire' attachment as it can be used without the comb. Remember to finish and tuck all the wires away safely if this is the method you wish to use.

Using the same wires, attach the corsages to the comb. You may not need the stay-wire joined in if you are using the comb, but it does help to stabilize the two corsages.

Support and protect the flowers on the front of the comb, then turn to the back and tuck in any loose wires and cover with tape. Turning back to the front, adjust the flowers to close any gaps.

Attach one end of the wired seashells to one end of the flowers, then wind in and around the flowers securely before finishing at the other end, and tuck the wire into the flowers to prevent it catching on the hair.

Finally, box, mist with water, cover with cellophane and keep in a cool place until needed.

Two matching corsage shapes ready for assembly on comb.

Joining two corsages together with wires.

Back of comb showing the attached wires.

Back of comb showing tape covering the wires.

Adding seashells to the comb.

Circlet Headdress

Circlet, garland, crown or wreath headdress are all names for a circle of flowers that fits around the circumference of the wearer's head. You can add flowers and foliage to them in a regular pattern or for a more natural look they can be added at random. But whichever style you choose they must be balanced around the design and not be heavier on one side than the other.

MATERIALS
Guide to flowers and foliage (exact quantities will vary with different headdress sizes):

7 lisys
7 roses
5 ivy leaves
5 rose leaves
5 hellebore
5 clematis seed heads
5 ivy seed heads
Wires for taping
Tape
2 x 20swg (0.90mm) stub wires
1 x 30swg (0.32mm) green-coated wire
Stem wrap
Tape measure

METHOD
Using 2 x 20swg (0.90mm) stub wires, mould into a circle to the required size and twist together. Tape with stem wrap. Cut the 30swg (0.32mm) green wire into two pieces and bend to create two loops. The loops are used for securing hairgrips to the head; additional loops can be added for extra security if needed.

Discard damaged flowers and leaves, then wire and tape each flower, seed head and leaf separately. Lay them out in sequence of application.

Take one flower or leaf at a time, and join them in by taping $1^1/_2$ " (4cm) of the wired stems separately to the wired circlet, moving along each time to give

A circlet of roses, lisys, seed heads and leaves.

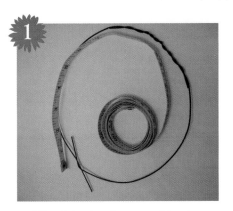

Wires joined and measured for size.

Wired circlet taping plus two hairgrip loops.

Prepared flowers.

Start adding flowers.

The inside of the circlet showing the taping.

The completed circlet.

until needed. Make sure any surplus water is removed before placing the circlet onto the head.

Natural Twig or Vine Designs

Natural plant materials can be used to create many shapes and designs or used as caging to support flowers and foliage. To mould these mediums into shape, fresh stems or twigs retaining sap must be used to give flexibility, otherwise the twigs and vines will be rigid and snap.

Natural Twig Heart

MATERIALS
Flexible twigs (silver birch is used here)
Tulips
Pennycress
Grape hyacinth
Fine gauge reel wire
Ribbons

METHOD
Gather twigs and vines while they are fresh, then strip off foliage and awkward-shaped branching offshoots.

Straighten the twigs and lay them parallel. Join in and secure the reel wire, leaving it on the reel. Bind additional twigs into the structure, moving along the shape until the desired length is achieved. Bind firmly but not too tightly, as the flowers will need to be poked into the wire and twig framework.

Bind another length of twigs to match the first.

Join and bind the two twiggy structures into a heart shape and secure the ends with the wire.

Make sure all the chosen flowers have been conditioned well as they will not have access to water once added to the frame. Wedge each flower into the twig structure and twist the existing reel wire around the stem to secure; additional wiring may be needed for extra security. Seasonal flowers on a cool spring

space for the next. Trimming the excess wired stems as you travel around the circle will give a neater and lighter finish to the circlet. At intervals around the circlet, tape in the two hairgrip loops as you go.

Close up, showing the position and taping of the hairgrip loops and the

length of stem left proud of the circlet.

Now you have a completed circlet with its inside taping showing. At this point, flowers and leaves can be adjusted slightly to correct the positioning.

Now you can box and mist with water, cover with cellophane, and keep cool

A natural twig heart.

1 Trimming twigs.

2 Wire into shape.

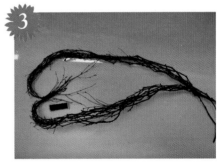

3 Bind together.

4 Inserting flowers.

afternoon will only last the day at most. To make flowers last longer, use a vial to put the cut stems into then wire onto the frame (this is essential when using summer flowers). Finally, mist with water and keep in a cool place until needed.

Tip: Plastic or glass vials can be wired into garlands to keep flowers supplied with water.

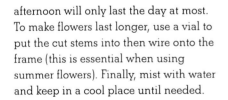

Vial containing water and rose.

Natural Vine Circlet

MATERIALS

Clematis vines
Bluebells
Hyacinth pips

Green, cotton-covered wire
Decorative bullion wire

METHOD
Select the soft, pliable ends of the vine
and trim all unwanted foliage and hard
stems.

  Form the vines into the required size of
circle, and secure with green cotton-
covered wire. Add the flowers around
the circlet, binding each one with
bullion wire to keep in place. Then box,
mist with water, cover with cellophane,
and keep cool until needed.

Garlands

Simple green garlanding is lightweight,
flexible and can be used pinned to
tablecloths to enhance the top and cake
tables, or wound around pillars, stairs,
gates, the inside of marquees and the
backs of chairs. This versatile type of
decoration can be constructed in several
ways. For example, long lengths of plant
material can be joined together to make
longer lengths, or short lengths of
flowers and foliage can be bound onto
rope, cord or ribbon. Evergreen foliage
such as ivy and ruscus is good to use, as
it will stay fresh for the duration of the
wedding. If you are including flowers
make sure they are hardy and well
conditioned so will survive without
water for a few hours at least. Garlands
made in long sausages of caged floral
foam will keep flowers fresh but this
method is much heavier and more
labour-intensive.

A natural vine circlet.

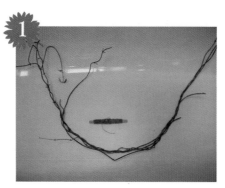
. Trim vine.

Shape the circlet to size.

Simple Green Garland

MATERIALS
4 long stems of soft ruscus (5′, 152 cm x
3′, 91cm table)
Green reel wire
4 elastic bands
4 safety pins
4 bows

Measure the length of the table,
allowing extra for the 'swag'. If the
garland is to be used for a table, wash or
at least check the foliage is clean before
pinning to a white tablecloth.

METHOD
Lay two pieces of ruscus parallel to each
other and join together the growing tips
with an 8″ (20cm) overlap by winding
green reel wire around the two pieces.
Secure the wire, making sure all loose
ends are neatly worked in to avoid
possible snagging.

Take another piece of ruscus and join
the two hard stem ends together with an
elastic band and add a safety pin.
Repeat for the other end of the table.

The flexibility of rubber bands can be
used to allow stretching when the two
ends are pulled into position.

Tie the bows around the corner and
attach to the tablecloth.

A simple green garland (front elevation).

Greenery, pins, wire, rubber bands and bows.

Two ends of growing tips.

The flexibility of rubber bands; adding safety pins.

Add bows to corners and pin to tablecloth.

Flower Garland Bound onto String

MATERIALS
Small spray rose buds
Small pieces of hydrangea
Fern
String
Wire
Ribbon

METHOD
Measure the length of rope needed for the garland, including extra for the swag and for the two ends that will need to overlap and be joined, plus more for making attachment loops. Estimate how many flowers and pieces of foliage you will need to complete the whole length by placing them out along the string.

Cut the length of rope into two pieces and cut all the flowers and foliage into suitable sizes, leaving some stem for attaching. Make a loop at each end of the two lengths of rope for attaching to the tablecloth or tying onto chairs. Wire each flower and piece of foliage on separately, to the required length. Repeat for the second piece of rope.

When each side is complete, turn over and wire the two rope ends together, then neaten the cut wire to avoid snagging.

Tie ribbon bows into loops and tie to the chair or table.

A flower garland wired onto string.

String, wire and flowers.

Two ends of string are left for joining.

Wiring two ends together.

A garland tied to a chair.

Streamers

Streamers can be made with all types of plant material and added to bridal designs, flower arrangements or just left hanging free. Streamers can add colour and texture, and can create interest and add length and movement to static designs.

Streamer

MATERIALS
Any plant material that will last out of water for the day
   Any wire that is suitable to take the weight of the used plant material (bullion wire if your arrangement is light and dainty)

METHOD
Take a few rose petals at a time and roll them up.
   Leave the wire on the roll and start a few inches (centimetres) along. This will give you an end for attaching onto the

Birdcage with streamer.

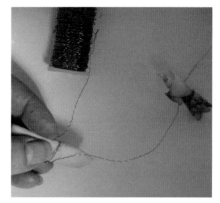

Rolled rose petals.

design. Bind the wire around the petals and give it a final twist to secure before moving onto the next item. You can make the space between each item as long or short as you like.
   Wire the stems of other selected flowers and buds into streamers for further interest and contrast. You can make each of the streamers with one flower or alternate with different buds and plant material on the same wire.

Binding with wire.

Chapter 7

Bouquets

Hand-tied bouquets are constructed with flowers and foliage that are then held in the hand on natural stems. The stems radiate out and are tied at one main point which then becomes the handle. The handle should be made light and comfortable to hold. A good balance should be maintained without the bouquet falling sideways, backwards or forwards. This can be achieved by adding the largest or heaviest flowers close to the centre or evenly distributed throughout the design. Visual balance can also be created with a variety of colours, sizes and textures. Either alternate these evenly within the bouquet or balance these elements with equal eye-pull so that one is not dominant over another on opposite sides of the bouquet. If this happens, the design will look lopsided. The tying point is finished with ribbon, decorative wires, raffia, lace or string. Depending on the style of bouquet the stems are either spiralled or parallel. Collars of leaves and other plant material can be added as well as beads

and decorative accessories. All plant materials should be clean and undamaged. Ensure none of the material is toxic and that it will not stain clothing.

The expression 'hand-tied' can signify a round, asymmetrical or cascading bouquet. Round bouquets, which are viewed all around and carried with two hands at the front of the dress, can be loosely tied, compactly tied or with a variety of texture. Asymmetrical bouquets can also be classed as loose when the flowers and foliage are soft and flowing, and compact when all the flowers are close together. Asymmetrical, or over-the-arm bouquets are viewed from one side only as they are carried across the body and over the crook of the elbow. Cascading, sheaf, shower and waterfall hand-tied bouquets are viewed from the front and sides and are made to look natural and spontaneous. Such designs have a certain degree of elegance, volume and spaciousness. These bouquets are held with two hands in front of the dress with elbows slightly crooked, thus allowing the flowers to

flow down naturally in front of the dress.

Storing

Finished bouquets can be stored using a tissue paper collar to protect the flowers and their stems. Keep them in water in a cool room out of any draughts and sunlight until required. Extra support will be needed for the length of sheaf, shower and waterfall bouquets. All stems should be wiped dry before handing to the bride.

The flowers used in the following step-by-step instructions have been selected to show clarification, clean lines and design. By substituting and combining contrasting materials in various textures, forms, colours and stem lengths, you will create a bouquet that has very different characteristics, but the basic method of assembly stays the same. There is such a wide selection of flowers and plant material to choose from, it is up to you (and the bride!) to decide on the look you wish to create.

LEFT: Traditional shower bouquet.

Round Hand-Tied Bouquet with Aspidistra Leaf Collar

This is a clean, neat and classy bouquet where every piece of plant material is clearly seen. Only choose the best-quality roses and undamaged leaves for the bouquet to look its best.

MATERIALS
12 large-headed roses
8 aspidistra leaves
Pot tape
Double-sided tape
Pearl-headed pins
Leaf shine
Satin ribbon
Flower scissors

METHOD
Once you have started to hold and assemble the bouquet you will only have one hand free, so gather all tapes, ribbons and pins together before you start.

Condition roses and check for and remove any damaged petals. Then defoliate and remove all thorns and lay the flowers out on a workbench. Clean the aspidistra leaves and spray with leaf shine, then lay them out with the roses.

Start by holding one flower stem in your left hand.

Using your right hand, introduce one flower at a time over the stem of the previous one. Keep turning the bouquet in your hand in the same direction each time another flower is added. This

Hand-tied bouquet with aspidistra collar.

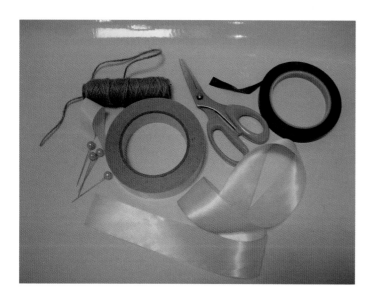

Materials for hand-tied bouquet with foliage surround.

Prepared roses and aspidistra leaves.

First steps for assembling the bouquet.

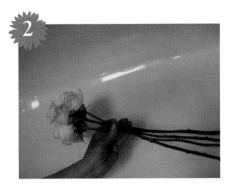

Turning the flowers in the hand to a neat finish.

Tie and secure the stems.

Adding aspidistra leaves around the roses.

Binding all the stems together.

Cutting the stems to length.

should create spiral stems. No stems should cross each other.

Keep turning and adding the rose heads close together until the bouquet has a domed appearance. Then secure the stems firmly at the tying point.

Add the aspidistra leaves one at a time by folding them in half and presenting them at the tying point until all of the roses are surrounded. Adjust the leaves accordingly, as they will not all be exactly the same size. They should form a collar.

Bind with pot tape to secure the stems and leaves, but do not make this area too thick and bulky or you will not have a neat, straight handle.

Bind the stems with double-sided tape and wind the satin ribbon over the tape to form the handle. Fold the satin ribbon over the cut end to give a neat finish. Insert the pearl-headed pins through the ribbon in an upward movement and through the stems, making sure the pins do not protrude out of the other side.

Firmly hold the stems of the bouquet and cut straight across.

Hand-Tied Bouquet with Natural Flower Collar

Before you start assembling this style of bouquet make sure you have enough pieces of plant material (flowers or foliage) cut and trimmed to size to fit all the way around the finished design.

Loose Hand-Tied Posy Bouquet

Choose a selection of flowers in different shapes and sizes. Some will stick out from the bouquet and others will be recessed. Therefore, the heads of each flower will not be at the same level and a more natural, loose look will be achieved. This design is sometimes called a 'freshly picked' bouquet.

MATERIALS
Cornflowers
Delphiniums
Feverfew
Sea lavender
Marigolds
Zinnia
Wheat
Scabious
Ribbon
Tie

METHOD
Condition all flowers and check them over for any damage. Gather your ribbons, bows and ties. Strip all leaves from flowers that will fall below the tying point, then sort the cleaned flowers and place these in separate groups on the table. Start the bouquet by holding one flower stem across another, using your left hand for holding and your right hand for inserting more stems. (Reverse this if you are left-handed.)

Turn the bouquet to the left and present another flower across the two previous stems (shown here is a pink zinnia).

Turn the bouquet to the left and add another flower over the previous stems.

Hand-tied bouquet with flower collar.

Loose hand-tied posy bouquet.

Flowers ready for making posy bouquet.

Holding stems in the first placement.

Showing the pink zinnia flower.

Continuing to add more flowers.

Tie the stems securely.

Cut the stems to length to make the handle.

Add a bow at the tying point to cover tape.

Standing hand-tied loose posy bouquet.

Turn the bouquet to the left and insert another flower (shown here is a blue scabious). Keep turning the bouquet to the left, adding one more stem each time until all the flowers are inserted. You can reposition a flower by loosening your grip slightly and pulling out the flower, adding it in again in the new position, then tightening your grip again.

Tie off the stems, before holding them firmly together and cutting off the surplus length. A good proportion is one third of the total length of the bouquet overall.

Lay the bouquet down and present the bow at the tying point.

Take the two tails ends of the bow and wrap them around the back of the bouquet. Then bring the tail ends back to the front of the bouquet and tie two or three knots over the top of the bow. Keeping the knot above the bow and nearest the flowers ensures it is comfortable to hold and out of the way.

The bouquet should now stand alone on its stems if good balance has been achieved. The pink zinnia is seen in the middle, creating visual balance, as it is dominant both in colour and size.

Compact Hand-Tied Bouquet

Choose a selection of flowers with heads of a similar form, where the heads can be made to sit approximately at the same level. When the flower heads are closely arranged together the profile of the bouquet should form a dome shape. The stems are assembled in the same way as loose hand-tied bouquets.

Textured Hand-Tied Bouquet

By choosing flowers, foliage, berries and seed heads with different textures, both on the surface area of the flowers and leaves and as perceived by the eye, you could create interesting and unusual bouquets. Follow the same instructions as for loose hand-tied bouquets.

Textured hand-tied bouquet.

Compact hand-tied bouquet.

Hand-Tied Sheaf Bouquet

MATERIALS

'Pretty Wendy' aster (aka September
flower)
Larkspur
Peonies
Lisy
Stock
Roses
House-leek flower heads
Tie
Pot tape
Raffia
String

METHOD

Condition all flowers and foliage and
check for any damage. Gather all
ribbons, bows, string, ties and tape.
Remove all thorns from the roses and
defoliate all flowers and foliage that fall

Hand-tied sheaf bouquet.

Flowers laid out ready for assembly.

First steps for making sheaf bouquet.

Adding flowers one by one.

below the tying point; this area will form
the handle. Place your flowers and
foliage on a workbench in groups. Next,
hold one of the longest flowers or pieces
of foliage in your left hand at a point
down the stem that will form the overall
length of the finished design. Use your
right hand to hold the stems if you are
left-handed. This position should now
be held constant throughout the
creation process. Flowers and foliage
with strong stems are the best to use

here, as they will form a support on
which to lay the rest of the flowers.

Using your right hand, start adding
flowers and foliage over the stems to the
left side of the bouquet, and under the
stems from the right side.

Large focal flowers are laid down
straight in the centre of the design; this
will create visual and actual balance.
Continue to add flowers, left over, right
under and focal flowers straight, until
the design is finished.

Placing in the central blooms.

Tying the stems to secure the bouquet.

You can reposition any flower by loosening your grip and sliding the flower out and in again. Remember that the stems must never cross. When you are happy with the design, tie the stems firmly and bind with pot tape, turning the tape with the sticky side uppermost on the last turn; this will help any ribbon or string finish to adhere to it (or if this proves too bulky, double-sided tape may be used). Without this, you could find the bouquet becomes loose and falls apart.

If there are a lot of stems, as with this bouquet, you may find the handle becomes bulky. Cutting the stems into a triangle to reflect the shape of the design will thin the handle and make it easier to hold. If the stems form a

Finish the sheaf bouquet with a raffia bow for a country-garden look.

slimmer finish you may wish to cut them straight across. Either way, a good proportion is one third of the overall length of the design, or one and a half widths of the bride's hand.

Secure the bow by wrapping the tail ends around the tying point, covering the tape and bringing the ends back to the front to tie off over the bow.

Loose Sheaf Bouquet

For the method of assembly follow all the instructions for the hand-tied sheaf bouquet, but remember that the plant material chosen here is longer and of a more flowing nature. The form of the foliage will, by its very nature, flow into an informal natural style with some fine trimming.

Asymmetrical Over-the-Arm, Hand-Tied Bouquet

Follow the instructions for the hand-tied

Compact, over-arm, hand-tied bouquet.

Loose, over-arm, hand-tied bouquet.

Loose, hand-tied, sheaf bouquet.

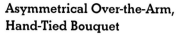

sheaf bouquet, but add more flowers and light foliage to flow over the right-hand side of the design if the bouquet will be held over the left arm, or add more flowers to the left-hand side if it is to be carried over the right arm. The side held nearest to the chest should remain flat so flowers are not crushed and there is no damage to the dress.

Hand-Tied Bouquet with Framed Collar

MATERIALS
20 large rose heads with buds
Small pieces of ivy to cover the frame
Little twiglets of birch
Length of aluminium or pliable wire to form the frame
4 stub wires, 18swg (1.25mm)
Stem wrap

Hand-tied bouquet with ivy collar.

Materials laid out ready for assembling bouquet with ivy collar.

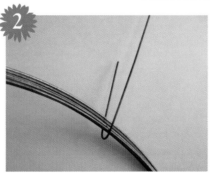

First, make the wire frame and add wires for handle.

Bending wires to form the handle.

Bending the handle wires and taping to secure.

Tie in the ivy trails and small twigs all around the frame.

One by one add the roses to form a compact domed shape.

Brown paper-covered wire
Ribbon for the handle
Tie or pot tape for securing the stemmed handle

METHOD
Make the frame first by creating a shape with several circles of the aluminium wire, then secure this with paper-covered wire. This one measures 9″ (23cm) across and 27″ (69cm) around.

Attach the four stub wires at equal distances around the frame by making a hook to go over the aluminium wire. Secure in place with stem wrap, covering all the way down the stub wire.

Take all four stub wires across the centre of the circle and, where they meet in the middle, bend them down vertically to form the handle.

Using the brown paper-covered wire, attach the twigs and ivy trails evenly around the framework. Make sure all the ends of the wires are neat and trimmed and concealed from the perimeter of the frame to avoid snagging.

Add the roses to the frame by slotting them in and around each quarter between the wires in a spiralled manner, as for a hand-tied design. The shape will be a little irregular due to the varying heights of the rose blooms to their buds. As the stems of the roses will be thick, especially with the added wires, tie off and secure the stems with pot tape, as this gives more strength to the tying point. Cut to the required length and finish the bouquet with ribbon, making sure that all the pot tape is concealed.

Foam Bouquet Holder

Posy holders are made with plastic handles, many of which are white and can become sweaty and slippery with nervous hands. Covering the handles with ribbon or leaves will make them more comfortable to handle and help them blend in with the colours and

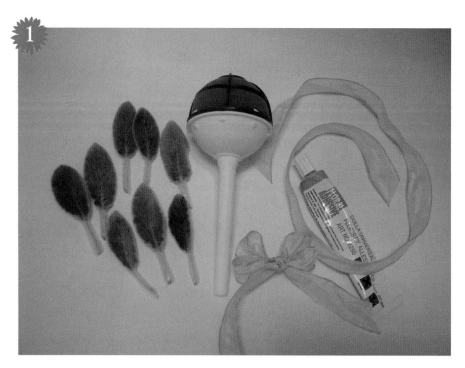

Cover the bouquet holder to conceal the plastic frame.

textures of the flowers in the bouquet or with the fabric of the dress.

MATERIALS
Leaves
1 posy holder
Double-sided tape
Ribbon
Cold glue

METHOD
Select a suitable size of posy holder to complement the style of and accommodate the flowers you have chosen for the bouquet. Gather enough leaves to encircle the white plastic base of the posy holder.

Trim the stalks off the leaves and grade them to ensure they are all the

same length. With cold glue, stick on one leaf at a time. They should be neat and slightly overlapping.

Stick double-sided tape to the handle.

Starting at the base of the cage of the posy holder, and leaving a length of ribbon at the top, wind the ribbon down over the double-sided tape.

Apply a very small amount of glue at the bottom of the handle, just to hold the ribbon in place before winding it back up to the top. Take care to cover all the white plastic, then cut off the ribbon, leaving a small amount to tie in the bow.

Make a small ribbon bow and, with the two ends of winding ribbon left at the top, tie firmly under the base of the posy holder, catching in all the stem ends of the leaves.

Gluing on leaves.

Glued leaves around the bouquet top.

Glue the ribbon handle to secure.

Finish by adding a small bow at the top.

Medium-Size Shower Bouquet in Foam Bouquet Holder

MATERIALS
10 white lisy flower blooms plus a few buds
11 roses
1 open peony
16 pieces of variegated ivy for the outline
Small pieces of ivy to fill the centre
Prepared posy holder
Stub wires

METHOD
Condition and prepare all the flowers and foliage, checking for damage and discarding if necessary, before

Traditional shower bouquet.

Wire in trailing plant material for security.

Secure wire over the top of the bouquet cage.

Making an outline with foliage.

Adding the first flowers to reinforce the outline.

Place the largest flowers in the centre of the bouquet.

reaching a peak at the centre of the bouquet (the centre is a third from the top, leaving two-thirds to flow downwards), and finishing with the peony. Lastly, add small pieces of ivy into and around the centre flowers to fill any gaps. Finally, box, mist with water, cover with cellophane and keep in a dark, cool, draught-free place until needed.

Pomanders

Although pomanders have been around since the thirteenth century and the name derived from the French *pomme*

A pretty pomander.

defoliating and removing thorns from the roses. Cut the foliage into lengths: use long pieces for trailing down, medium lengths for the bottom sides and short pieces for around the top of the bouquet, with very short pieces for filling in the centre. Grade the lisys and roses in the same way, leaving the peony for the centre. Mist the floral foam of the posy holder until damp but not dripping with water.

Tip: Laying your flowers and foliage out on the workbench in as close to the finished shape as possible will help with the order of assembly.

Wire the longest trails of ivy with a single mount. Push the wire up from the bottom of the holder until it protrudes from the top. Bend the wire to form a hairpin and push back down into the

top of the foam, catching over the plastic cage structure. Make sure the wire connected to the stem of the ivy is pulled back up into the foam so it is out of view. Repeat with as many of the trails of ivy as will fall in a downward direction that may be vulnerable to falling out.

Create the outline shape with ivy, wiring in as many pieces as is necessary to hold them in place.

Insert the lisys into the foam, following the outline shape. Again if the stems are trailing, wiring them in will give more security.

Insert the roses, longest one first, following the shape of the bouquet, then add the centre peony. If the longest roses are heavy you may like to wire them in. As you work your way up the bouquet the flowers should be placed in to form a profile (making a dome shape),

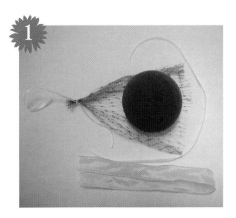

Securing the floral foam sphere with netting.

Adding the handle ribbon to a pomander.

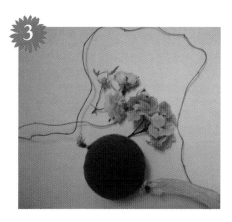

Add the first flowers to the pomander to create shape.

Adding more flowers evenly all around.

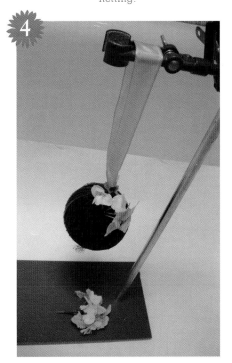

Filling in with the rest of the plant material.

Adding vines to create extra interest.

d'ambre we tend to associate them with the English Tudor period because of the many paintings showing pomanders being carried or worn hanging from clothes. Today we have adapted the pomander's use so it can be carried by brides and bridesmaids. Pomanders are sphere-shaped designs of flowers and plant material carried by a ribbon or

Pomander

MATERIALS
Small rose buds
Spriglets of hydrangea
1 foam sphere
Garden netting
Tie
Ribbon

METHOD
Cut the garden netting to size to fit over

cord-looped handle. They must be lightweight and made a size that is appropriate to the intended carrier. Long-lasting flowers should be used for this design as water supply to the stems is limited.

the foam sphere, allowing extra length at both ends for tying. Tie the ends very tightly as some young bridesmaids may well treat the flower ball unsympathetically! Tie the ribbon loop to one of the ends.

Hang the pomander on a florist's bouquet stand or improvise with a chair back or doorknob. Mist the pomander with water, but do not soak it, as this will make it very heavy and it will drip with water.

Using one hand to steady the sphere,

distribute the flowers evenly around the ball. Make sure you push all the stems in as far as you can to secure them. If you can, make the heads of the flowers come into contact with the damp foam. Flowers left on stalks that are too proud will become vulnerable to breaking.

Adding trailing vines, beads, ribbons or decorative wires can create extra interest.

If the vine is sturdy enough it can be poked into the pomander to secure it, otherwise attach it with a hairpin wire. Add the vine by winding it over and around the flowers before securing. Finally, box, mist with water and keep in a cool place until needed. Make sure there is no surplus water on the surface of the flowers that may transfer to clothes.

Bridesmaid's Rustic Jam-Jar Posy

Small, dainty field and garden flowers are perfect for a little bridesmaid's jam-

Jam jar filled with country flowers for a small bridesmaid.

jar posy, but these are only recommended to be carried on soft ground such as meadows, lawns and inside marquees. Make sure the ribbon loop is firmly secured.

Natural, Rustic Bark Trug

Bark is useful here, not only because of its pliable nature, but because it can easily be found on the woodland floor, and is harmonious to woodland wedding themes. Don't forget to ask permission from the landowner if you are foraging for bark and also consider the many insects that may have made it their home. Bark can also be sourced from florist and craft outlets. These pieces will have been cleaned, flattened into square sheets and be ready to use. When worked into designs, bark is very lightweight and easy to handle for young bridesmaids. If it should accidentally get damaged, a little piece of bark coming off will not ruin the shape of the design.

MATERIALS
Silver birch bark
Bluebells
Dried mushrooms
Floral foam
Ribbon
Cold glue

Natural tree bark for making containers.

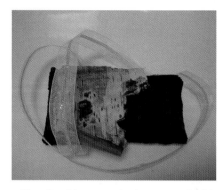

Glue floral foam inside the trug and add a ribbon handle.

Bluebells added to the bridesmaid's trug.

METHOD
Select a piece of bark that has retained the shape of the trunk of the tree. Make sure it is cleaned and any rough, twiggy offshoots are trimmed to avoid snagging – choose only the very soft outside pieces. As bluebells are notorious for wilting, a small piece of floral foam fitted inside the bark and glued into position will keep them hydrated. Spray the floral foam with water until damp, but not soaking wet; this will keep the bluebells fresh for the duration of the wedding and longer. Roll the bark over to close the opening and tie with the ribbon, leaving two loops to create the handle. Glue a few dried mushrooms to the top of the trug for added interest.

Condition the bluebells with a long drink of water and flower food. Cut the flower heads to fit into the floral foam on one side of the trug, and the stem ends to fit into the other side. Although the stems are usually kept long in this trug for effect, I would recommend that they are cut shorter for a young bridesmaid. Mist the bluebells with water but do not water the floral foam, and keep cool until needed.

Wedding Cake Flowers

The wedding cake is important to the rites and rituals of a marriage and takes pride of place on a separate table in a prominent position at the wedding breakfast. Wedding cakes are mentioned as far back as Roman times when the 'cake' (a sort of bread or biscuit containing barley) was broken over the heads of the bride and groom. Fruit and seeds in the cake were seen to be symbols of fertility and prosperity, and cutting the cake together was a sign of the couple's union. There is no record of when flowers first decorated wedding cakes, but it could simply be that a confectioner made sugar flowers to show off his/her skill. Making sugar flowers is time-consuming even with an experienced hand, so quite expensive. The use of real flowers to decorate a cake may have come about as a cheaper alternative or in war years when sugar was rationed. Some fresh flowers are edible and safe to use directly on the cake, including roses, violets, marigolds, pinks, daisies, chrysanthemums, lavender and rosemary. Only use flowers from the garden or a commercial outlet; flowers from the countryside may have been sprayed with insecticide or trampled by cattle. All flowers must be carefully cleaned and checked for wildlife. They can be washed in cold salt water and dried before being laid directly on a cake. They add colour, texture and, if eaten, flavour; they may also match the colours and theme of the

Tiered wedding cake sprinkled with small, colourful flowers.

wedding to complete the scene. Poisonous foliage and flowers should never be used on a cake even if they are only for decoration.

Tiered Flower Cake

Wedding cakes are usually delivered to the reception venue shortly before the bride and groom and all their guests arrive. This keeps the cake fresh and out of harm's way. The icing should be hardened off beforehand, whether it is royal or the sugar-paste type. The following method can only be used if the cake comes with all the tiers separated. The floral foam insertions are used to support and stack the cake into tiers, but only if the cake is lightweight and does not need dowels for stability. Check with the baker before you begin. For heavier cakes with dowels in place and a larger gap between the tiers as needed for bigger blooms, you can use two plastic-based rings. Place them with their foam together, one on top of the other, on cake boards between each layer. Decorating any cake with fresh flowers can only be done *in situ*. Make sure the cake and cake table are secure and stable before adding flowers. Do not mist the flowers with water even if the cake is placed by a hot, sunny window. It is better to have less than perfect perky blooms than a wet cake. If necessary, give caterers advice on deconstructing the cake before cutting and serving to guests.

Tiered wedding cake stuffed with pink hydrangea.

MATERIALS

5 or 6 hydrangea heads
2 floral foam cushion shapes with hard foam bases, one to fit within the inside of the top tier with space for the flowers, and one to fit the size of the bottom tier
A small plastic container fitted with floral foam for the top.
Cellophane

METHOD

Cut two pieces of cellophane to the shape of each of the tiers of cake, and lay over the icing for protection against water damage. Cut through the solid base of each of the floral foam shapes. Then lightly mist with water.

Make a sandwich with the floral foam, with one hard piece on the bottom and the other cut piece on the top of the wet floral foam. The solid pieces will prevent the tiers of the cake collapsing. (Cakes with more than two tiers may need the support of dowels and cake boards.)

Cut little springlets of hydrangea and insert into the floral foam until all the foam is covered.

Mist the floral foam in the container for the top of the cake and add more hydrangea pieces.

Cutting the floral foam to fit each tier of the cake.

Lightly misting with water.

Placing each slice of foam into the cake.

Adding hydrangea florets.

Make a small posy for the top of the cake.

Chapter 8

Techniques for Creating Wedding Styles in Floral Foam

Designing with floral foam allows you to use plant material in many ways to create floral arrangements suitable for wedding work. Whether choosing traditional, European or freestyle arrangements (see the following examples for details), the floral foam will hold stems in position and at the same time keep any plant material supplied with water. The advantages with this are that small arrangements can be made in advance and delivered to the venue, and larger designs can be worked on *in situ* several days before the wedding, thus allowing more time to work on the bridal bouquets, headdresses, corsages and buttonholes that require preparation closer to the day.

Traditional Arrangements

The 'traditional' label is given because this is a massed style developed before the sparse styles of the 1950s. Foliage grown in British gardens was used extensively for many of these arrangements both by the florist and flower-arranger, mainly due to the lack of variety of commercially grown greenery.

Traditional arrangement characteristics:
- All the stems appear to radiate from a point in the centre of the container.
- Plant material that is smaller in form yet longer in stem is used for the outline framework.
- Flowers are graded in size from top to bottom and sides to the centre of the arrangement.
- The largest flowers and leaves with shorter stems are placed centrally in the container to create a focus of interest, a recession, and to give a 3D effect.
- Usually mixed flowers and foliage are used.
- Flowers and foliage should vary in shape and texture.
- Flowers do not all face the same way. They should be turned to show different profiles.
- Space is created around each flower.

The following step-by-step arrangements are shown using easily identifiable flowers and foliage. Choosing plant material with alternative forms, lengths and textures creates a different look, but the principles of design are the same.

Table Centrepieces

If there is somewhere that needs to impress the most, the dining table displays are the place to create that 'wow' factor. Sitting around a table for several hours with stunning flowers in the middle can induce a talking point with guests and gain much admiration. Choice flowers can lift the occasion and tie together colours, themes, and improve the whole atmosphere bringing harmony to the wedding reception. But table designs should be looked at in proportion to the overall size of the table and setting. As a general guide, centrepieces should occupy one fifth to one third of the table size; anything under this size will appear skimpy and may be overlooked; anything over this size may overwhelm the table and guests making it look cluttered. The height of flower arrangements on dining tables should not exceed 12in (31cm), this enables diners to look across the table for conversation, or tall designs should be made above head height to allow a clear view under the display. Anything in between this will block the guests' view of each other and stop any interaction. Centrepieces should also complement the shape of the table, a round posy on a round table and a long and low arrangement on an oblong table. As the designs should look attractive from all angles and be viewed at close quarters, flowers and foliage should be clean, free from damage, in good condition, and not poisonous.

Guests with allergies should also be considered, as strongly perfumed flowers may cause irritation, a room full of highly scented oriental lilies can become overpowering, and hay fever sufferers can feel uncomfortable especially when types of grasses are used. Softer scents are given off with sweetpeas, lily-of-the valley, tuberose, hyacinths, stocks, lavender and some roses. Herbs such as rosemary, mint and thyme added in arrangements will smell fresh and may even complement the main dish!

Traditional Table Posy

MATERIALS
24 small pieces of myrtle
Small pieces of fern (e.g. Asparagus setaceus)
4 roses
3 standard carnations
1 pink gypsophila cut into sprigs
3 pink veronica, cut into smaller pieces
1 lilac lisianthus

A watertight container (the one shown here is an 8″ (20cm) glass fruit bowl)
Decorative paper for lining the bowl (to add colour and conceal the foam)

Floral foam to fit inside the bowl, cut to stand at least 3cm proud of the rim
Clear tape

Simple summer table posy.

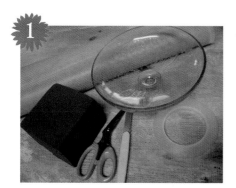

Ingredients for small posy.

Floral foam cut and secured in the bowl on top of decorative paper.

Myrtle inserted around the edge of the foam to establish shape.

4

Roses and carnations added to establish design.

Looking down on the position of the flowers.

METHOD

Cut the decorative paper to fit into the container, and place the floral foam in the centre. The chamfered (or bevelled) edges of the foam will discourage any surplus water from spilling over the edge of the container by directing it back into the bowl. Secure the floral foam into position with clear tape.

Insert small pieces of myrtle around the circumference of the foam at a slight upward angle and just overlapping the edge of the container to make the outline. Add one piece of myrtle standing upright near to the middle of the posy to establish height.

Insert one rose into the centre of the design and the remaining three roses at an equal distance apart, further down into the design. These will be the focal flowers (which have been chosen in a light colour here to show positioning). Add the three carnations in between the three roses, at an equal distance apart.

Now the shape has been established with the main flowers, you can distribute all the other flowers in and around the posy at an equal distance apart within the outline shape. All the flowers and foliage should radiate from one point.

Mist with water and store in a cool place until needed.

Small Cupcake Posy

MATERIALS
1 stem of spray carnations
1 stem of spray roses
7 stems of loosestrife
3 spray chrysanthemum flowers
A few small sprigs of myrtle
Cake cup ready with floral foam

Cupcake collection.

1

Adding flowers to establish height for the cupcake.

2

Cupcake made with small flowers.

METHOD
Wet the floral foam inside the cake cup. Add one central flower to create height and fill in with the rest of the flowers, as with the table posy.

Traditional Long and Low Table Design

This design traditionally sits on the top table for a wedding, but can be used to fit any long or oval table. Top tables on average are 24' (600cm) in length and seat eight to ten people, but not all reception venues have a uniform size. It is always advisable to establish the number of people who will be sitting at the top table; this will give an indication of overall length. The design should be positioned central to the bride and groom on the outside edge of the table. As the couple is the centre of attention and many photos are taken here, it would be prudent to make this display with care, using the showiest and best-quality flowers. The design shown here is 31" (80cm) long and has a soft, feminine outline.

Remember, the flower list provided next is only a guide; you can select flowers to match any chosen theme and/or colour. If the front edge of the table has space to be clearly seen, and if it won't impede passers-by or catering staff, the use of trailing foliage over the front edge of the table gives a soft, flowing effect down over the tablecloth. Select flowers and foliage in proportion to the size of the design you wish to create and the size of the table.

MATERIALS
4 medium pieces of griselinia foliage
4 medium pieces of cheesewood foliage
4 stems of lisianthus
1 stem of 'Pretty Wendy' aster (cut the side stems off to use as individual pieces)
4 peonies
9 roses
7 pieces of fountain grass
Shallow plastic tray container
Floral foam
Pot tape

METHOD
Cut the soaked floral foam to size, place in the tray and secure into position with pot tape, avoiding any crossing at the centre, as this is where the focal flower is placed.

Cut two of the longest pieces of foliage to the same size and insert into each end of the foam to establish the finished length. Use smaller pieces of foliage at the sides to create the width (in proportion to the width of the table).

Fill in the shape with additional foliage, leaving room for the flowers.

Traditional long and low table design.

Secure floral foam in a tray with pot tape.

Establish the length and width of your design with foliage.

Set out your overall shape with foliage.

Add September flower and lisianthus to the design.

Insert peonies into the centre of the design.

Finish the design by adding fountain grass.

Insert lisianthus and aster to follow the outline shape.

Add the largest flowers (peonies) raised up in the centre to create height and form the focal area, leaving a little space around each bloom.

Add the roses in the spaces between the peonies and lisianthus and finish with the fountain grass and any small pieces of aster and foliage.

Once all the floral foam is hidden from view, mist with water and store in a cool room until delivery.

Traditional Pew End/Spray

This design is made in foam and reflects the shape of the shower bouquet. Pew ends can also be made in an oval or round shape, which is especially useful if these are to be transferred to the reception for table centrepieces. Measure the length and width of the pew end and establish a method of attachment that won't damage the wood. Commercial pew-end mechanics can be purchased, but string, ribbon, wire or clips can be used as long as they are not too cumbersome or obtrusive. Take into consideration any decorative carving that may be obscured with a large design, and the width of the aisle.

MATERIALS
3 lengths of ivy or trailing foliage
2 pieces of trailing periwinkle foliage
Small pieces of myrtle
3 lisianthus
7 roses

Pew-end spray

Tray with secured floral foam.

Make an outline with foliage.

Add lisianthus to the outline.

Insert peonies in the middle of the design.

Finish by adding roses in between flowers.

3 peonies
Plastic tray with a handle
Floral foam
Pot tape
Ribbon or string

METHOD
Use a piece of ribbon long enough to thread through the hole of the handle and tie to the pew end. Pull the tails of the ribbon to meet evenly and tie a knot over the hole in the handle to stop the ribbon slipping. Next, cut the floral foam to size, soak it with water and secure it into the tray with pot tape running along the length and width of the foam. Then cross the tape, off centre, as this is where the focal flower will be placed.

Insert the trailing foliage up into the bottom end of the tray to set the length and establish an outline for the rest of the shape with shorter pieces of foliage. If making several pew ends with the same design, lay them side by side and make them all together, step by step, to ensure a consistent size and shape throughout.

Follow the outline of the foliage by adding lisianthus into the shape.

Add the peonies in the centre, a third from the top of the design, leaving two-thirds of the design to hang down. The profile should be in keeping the width of the aisle.

Fill in the design with the rest of the flowers, and add short pieces of foliage into any gaps to hide the floral foam. Pay attention to the sides of the tray, since the overall effect will be viewed while walking down the aisle. All the flowers should look as if they radiate out from the focal flower area.

Make sure the finished pew end is drained of surplus water before you tie it into position.

This design can be used to hang on gateposts, the pillars of a mandap for a Hindu or Jain wedding or the four corners of the chuppah for a Jewish wedding. Several sprays can be attached to a frame to make a floral arch.

Pedestal Arrangements
Pedestal arrangements are an assembly of flowers that are uplifted by placing on a stand or column. They can be designed in a triangle, round, oval or freestyle shape. Stands can be made from various metals, stone, ceramic, plastic, glass or wood. Finished designs can range in size and height up to 7' (213cm) for use in large halls or churches. Pedestal designs for cathedrals can be even taller when additional mechanics are applied. Churches will have their own pedestal stands, usually made of wrought iron, but sometimes you can find a wooden torchère stand; these are more decorative in style and would add further interest to the display. Whichever type of stand you choose should be in harmony with its setting, the arrangement size and the backdrop. All the mechanics in this design should be robust and stable enough to take the weight and, because of their size, are best worked on *in situ*. Wedding pedestals are only required to last for the duration of the ceremony and may not need maintenance, but if they are to be left for the regular worshippers to enjoy, leave room at the back of the floral foam for further watering.

A traditional pedestal is approximately 6' (184cm) tall and 4' (124cm) wide. For a good design you will need at least fifty

Floral foam secured in container with pot tape.

Traditional pedestal arrangement.

First placement of fern.

flowers of various shapes and sizes: long, spiky flowers for height and some outline; large, round focal flowers for recessing in the middle and medium-size flowers for filling in gaps.

MATERIALS
10 fern polystichum
5 lengths of trailing ivy
10 'Pretty Wendy' aster (aka September flower)
10 delphinium
10 stock
5 peonies

5 roses
5 white lisianthus
5 purple lisianthus
Large urn or stand
Container to fit inside the top of the urn
Two blocks of high-density floral foam, or a commercial pedestal block
Pot tape

METHOD
Soak and cut the floral foam to fit, leaving it at least 3″ (8cm) above the rim of the container; this will allow the ivy to flow down over the rim and connect with

Establish the outline shape with fern.

the urn to complete the picture. Avoid leaving a line between the flowers and container. Secure the foam with pot tape. Push all the stems into the floral foam as firmly as you can, or at least 3"

Add ivy flowing over the rim of the urn.

Include aster and delphiniums to create outline.

Fill in with more flowers.

Add stock into the design.

Include roses and peonies in the centre.

(8cm); this will help maintain the shape and prevent the collapse of the longer stems.

Add the fern upright; three-quarters of the way back into the foam.

Add the rest of the fern, establishing the outline.

Insert the stems of ivy in an upward direction, leaving it to flow down over the rim of the urn.

Add the September flower within the outline shape.

Add the delphiniums in some of the spaces.

Then evenly distribute the stock across the rest of the spaces

Insert the peonies and roses a little deeper into the centre of the arrangement to create recession.

All the stems should look as if they are radiating out from one central point. If the pedestal is to be positioned with its back to a wall or pillar, only a superficial amount of foliage will be needed to fill in the back and cover the floral foam. If, however, the back will be in any way exposed, you will need to add foliage and some flowers to the last third of the floral foam to create profile and a 3D effect. Once everything is in place, mist the flowers and top up the container with water.

Rings for Tables, Gates and Rims of Containers

Rings are available in sizes from 8″ (20cm) to 24″ (60cm) and can be used for many styles of table designs. Candles or a hurricane lamp can be added for a romantic feel. Taller pedestal arrangements can be stood in the centre of a ring, or they can be used as a surround for decorative birdcages. Rings and heart shapes also look very attractive when hung on doors, gates and on the rims of urns and containers.

MATERIALS

There are many types of foliage suitable for rings. The important thing is that what you choose is dense or compact with small leaves. Euonymus is used here and some other options are listed below; the required quantity of foliage will vary according to the size of the ring.

Buttercups
Cow parsley
Honesty
Rapeseed
A ring with a plastic base
A knife
Ribbon for hanging

METHOD

With a knife, trim the inside and outside of the foam ring, taking the angled

A ring of flowers on a garden gate. All the flowers were harvested from the field. A fine, dainty look is achieved by using small flowers.

Preparation of design by adding ribbon and trimming the edge of the foam.

Add foliage to the ring.

Flowers added to the ring.

107

edges away to create a rounded surface. Soak the ring by placing it in water upside down or by pouring water over the foam. If the ring is to be used on a table or elsewhere in the venue, do not saturate the foam, as any surplus water

Alternative ring design with floral streamers hanging from a rustic door.

Complete floral ring design.

Alternative design with candle and lamp.

will be displaced when the flowers are added, leaving water to seep out onto the tablecloth or floor. If the ring is to be hung outside on a door or gate, ribbon or string will need to be tied to the ring before inserting any plant material, and misting with water may be necessary to maintain freshness.

Cut the foliage into small pieces and insert into the foam, taking care to conceal all the plastic edges of the ring, both inside and outside, but leaving small spaces for the flowers.

Add the flowers into the foam aiming for a random effect but ensure they are evenly disbursed throughout.

Mist the ring with water and store in a cool room until needed.

Floral Arch

Decorating archways can be a massive undertaking and you will inevitably need help both with the mechanics and assembly on the day. Careful planning is required, including taking craftspeople to visit the site for measurements, perhaps across several visits. On the positive side, arches are undoubtedly the showiest of all the floral decorations, lending themselves to many photo opportunities and admiration. Once the arch (which is unique to each venue) is constructed, you can use it again, donate it to the venue or loan it out to another bride.

The details here were designed to fit a church doorway measuring 2.15m wide by 2.75m high, but to avoid protruding stonework, gargoyles, shoe scrapes etc., it actually finished 2.75m wide and 3m high, yet still some obstacles were unavoidable. There were only a few old, rusty nails embedded into the very top of the limestone to secure the frame, making the arch virtually self-supporting. The frame was made in sections for easy assembly, dismantling and transportation.

MATERIALS
Euonymus for covering the floral foam
250 cream roses
250 pink roses
3 pennycress
2 pieces of 4 x 4 wood (in this example the wood was measured and cut to fit under the stone gargoyles on the straight sides of the arch)
2 pieces of square (30m x 30m) 23ml plywood for the base
Paint
6 angle brackets with screws to fit
4 eyelets
20 screws
2 fibreglass rods (plumbing and plastic pipes can also be used)
Chicken wire
Garden wire

Church arch filled with roses.

22 blocks of floral foam
Pot tape
Wire-cutters
Ladders

METHOD
Join the plywood base to the 4 x 4 uprights by screwing angle brackets onto three sides of the bottom of each length, keeping the back clear to fit flat against the venue wall. Here, we also cut slots in the base wood to accommodate shoe scrapes, and painted all the wood green. Next, attach five screws down each side (outer and inner) of the length of the 4 x 4 at even intervals. This will give you fixing points for the chicken-wire cage. Now screw in the two eyelets

Wooden upright supports with base and angle brackets.

Floral foam wrapped in chicken wire.

Floral-foam chicken wire sections mounted on arch structure.

In situ floral foam blocks on side view with foliage.

Adding roses and pennycress foliage.

at the top of the length of each 4 x 4. These should be spaced vertically 3" (8cm) apart, for when you slot in the flexible fibreglass rods. Slot the rods into the eyelets and secure into position with garden wire. Next, cut lengths of chicken wire to fit the frame. Five lengths were cut for this frame. Fold over any sharp edges of chicken wire and cover with pot tape for safe handling. Soak floral foam blocks and lay these onto the length of chicken wire, then fold the chicken wire over and secure with garden wire by threading it through the holes and pulling tight. Now you can place the frame into position against the venue wall and secure it. Attach the cages to the frame of the arch with extra garden wire, using the screws on the inner and outer sides of the wooden supports. Add the foliage to the foam, leaving space for the flowers.

Add the roses randomly all over the arch, then add the pennycress for a little extra interest and profile.

Lychgate

Lychgates usually have several oak pillars holding up a small tiled roof, and are situated at the end of a church path next to the road. The stone bench in the middle of the gate is intended as a resting place for coffins on their way in and out of the church. Floral decorations here will announce to every passer-by that there is a wedding. In the following example, chicken-wire cages filled with

Lychgate design at All Saints' Church, Somerset.

Mechanics of assembly.

Side view of mechanics with foliage added.

floral foam were used and padded backing was attached to protect the oak from marking. The cages are tied to the beams with soft cotton cord to prevent damage. The flowers and foliage were added in at random, and the grasses were left long to create depth and texture. Care must be taken with lychgates not to overwater the foam, which may drip onto anyone passing beneath.

Lychgate design close-up.

Topiary Tree

Topiary trees are traditionally geometrically shaped hedging, and have been grown since Tudor times. The geometric shapes can be cubes, obelisks, pyramids, cones or spheres. Topiary trees have never been out of fashion for weddings and are still popular today both to flank doorways and on a smaller scale for table decorations. Traditional foliage for topiary trees is box, holly, yew, bay or myrtle, but as long as the foliage you choose is small and dense it can be used to create neat shapes. Ivy tops are a little more bulky and fill in the shape faster – they are also evergreen. Roses or daisies are harmonious with this design, but oranges, apples and berries would also be in keeping. The following instructions for topiary trees were designed to complement the period setting of the example wedding, and for ease of assembly, dismantling and transportation.

MATERIALS

Ivy
Roses
Apples
Metal frame (can be bought from garden centres or made bespoke by blacksmiths)
Plumber's plastic pipes (sourced from DIY stores) with two different diameters that will fit one into the other
Saw (to cut the pipes)
Quick-drying post cement
Container (used as a template to set the cement in)
Floral foam sphere (to fit inside the metal frame)
Small plastic dish (to sit the foam sphere in)
Suitable container or planter
Pot tape
Paper-covered wire (to secure ivy trails)
Stub wires (to hold the apples)
Paper
Rope
Double-sided tape

Topiary tree at Walton Castle, Somerset.

1

2

3

Topiary tree mechanics.

All pieces assembled, ivy being added.

METHOD
Cut a piece of the widest pipe to the height of the planter. Then, following the instructions on the cement packet, fix the short piece of pipe into the centre of the template container, making sure that it sits up vertically. You may need the aid of a spirit level. This pipe will hold the trunk of the tree so it is important to keep it straight.

Cut the smaller-diameter pipe to fit into the base pipe, to your chosen height. This will make the trunk of the tree. Next, cover the pipe with your selected medium. Paper is used here, stuck with double-sided tape and roped into position. Slot all sections of the topiary together and stand inside the planter. Now, gently prise open the metal topiary shape and insert the plastic dish with the wetted floral foam sphere. Return the shape of the metal back to its original form.

Add the foliage to cover the floral foam. Further trails of ivy can be bound around the outer frame and secured with wire to create more interest.

Add the roses.

Wire bunches of apples and secure them into the tree. Finally, stand the tree in position before misting with water.

4

Ivy tied in place.

5

Adding the feature flower into the design.

6

Close-up of a topiary tree with roses and apples.

Meadow Box

Meadow boxes are floral designs consisting of flowers found in fields and meadows that are arranged to imitate the growing pattern of plants. The aim is for it to look as natural as possible with flowers that all belong to one season. Flowers should be light, delicate and translucent, and grasses should sway gracefully in the slightest breeze. Meadow boxes can be made small to fit on tables or larger arrangements can be elevated on rustic boxes for use outside tents, yurts and barns where they blend harmoniously into the countryside. This style has been adopted from European floristry and has gained popularity in country wedding settings.

MATERIALS
Scabious
Cow parsley
Fountain grass
Poppy seed heads
Feverfew
A wooden box
Floral foam
Cellophane

METHOD
Cut sufficient cellophane to fit into the base of the box, with the cellophane reaching high enough up the sides to make the box watertight, then cut and fit the floral foam flat at the bottom of the box and soak it with water. Next, add flowers to the foam at random with all the stems in an upright position, just as they would grow in a meadow. A few bent pieces of grass will look natural, as if they had been trodden on by wildlife.

Meadow box.

Crate and floral foam for meadow box.

Floral foam inside crate.

European-Style Table Runner

Table runners can be used along the outer edge of the top table with the bridal party sitting on the opposite side, or they can be laid down the centre of the table with people sitting on both sides. Flowers and foliage should be kept relatively short so that interaction can take place across the table. This design has no central focal area; interest is created with a rhythmic movement of colours, textures and shapes of flowers and plant material.

Instructions for this table runner only cover one section to avoid unnecessary repetition, so repeat the same steps until the required length is achieved.

MATERIALS
6 pieces of Brachyglottis greyi (aka Senecio greyi) foliage
2 gypsophila
2 stems of spray carnations
5 white standard carnations

2 pink standard carnations
2 stems of chrysanthemums
5 roses
1 hydrangea cut into small florets

1 table tray 19″ (48cm) (already fitted

Cut flowers for table runner.

Tray with added foliage

Start adding flowers to the tray.

with floral foam – commercial table 'Deco' (Oasis) trays are strong, rigid and ready to use)

METHOD
Water the floral foam in the tray, then cut the foliage into small pieces and insert stems to cover most of the foam, leaving space for the flowers. Pay attention to the outer area of the design, making sure that all edges of the tray are concealed.

Cut the flower stems short and add to the runner; the white standard carnations are worked along the line in a staggered pattern, while the roses are inserted in an opposite stagger to the carnations. Finally, evenly distribute the remining flowers to fill the space.

Mist the runner and store in a cool place until needed.

Ice-Cream Tubs

Designs that use ice cream tubs and large bowls can be made with coloured floral foam, which when scooped out looks like real ice cream!

MATERIALS
Small rose buds
Hydrangea
Muehlenbeckia complexa
Ice-cream tub
Coloured foam
Spoon

METHOD
With the spoon, scoop out the floral foam into round portions and add to the tub. Add flowers.

Water and drizzle with Muehlenbeckia complexa.

Ice-cream design.

Ingredients for ice-cream design.

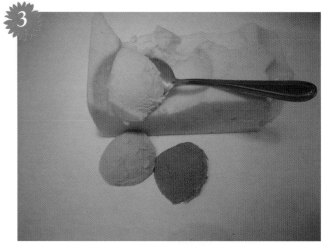

Scoop out floral foam with a spoon.

Adding floral foam to the tub.

Insert flowers and drizzle angel vine over the design.

Chapter 9

Summer

Summer provides a large number of seasonal pretty and perfumed flowers, especially roses. This is the month when roses are at their best, and are flowering profusely in our English gardens and countryside. Roses are still the most popular flower for weddings and our traditional buttonhole. There is an explosion of varieties of every size, shape and colour, except the ever-elusive blue. Blue roses can be sourced, but they are fed a blue dye in their water supply, colouring not only the petals blue but also their leaves, and your hands. Meanwhile, the petals of the dog rose growing in our country hedgerows may look alluring but are fragile. These blooms are best left until the autumn when their rose hips are much more valuable for use in floristry.

June has seen most of the spring flowers coming to an end, but peonies grown in French polytunnels then imported through Holland, along with Dutch field varieties, are available until July and should still be of good quality. Peonies are big, feminine and blousy and are a natural choice for bridal bouquets and other arrangements. Although available in white, cream, yellow and many shades of pink and deep crimson red, not all varieties will be available for the entire season.

Other summer flowers like delphiniums and larkspur have stronger, thicker and taller stems that will withstand arranging in floral foam without the stems bending and needing extra support, making them excellent flowers for immediate impact in large displays. Stocks in pink, purple and violet are wonderful for filling up a reception room with their sweet perfume, while sweet William, in white, pink and red, is a useful stabilizer in hand-tied bouquets and is great for adding texture. Dainty but thin-stemmed astrantia needs supporting in and among other flowers for hand-tied designs. Classic hydrangeas are now available with more than 100 different varieties to choose from. These are frequently grown and imported from the Netherlands.

Home-grown spring flowers have made way for moon daises, buttercups, grasses and cow parsley from our wild country meadows and waysides. English flower farms should now be harvesting the first crops of their wonderfully scented sweetpeas, a very quick and easy flower to fashion into a hand-tied posy, as there are no leaves to trim from the stems. There are too many summer flowers to list, and certainly enough to keep any bride happy. Indeed, we are now spoilt for choice! New growth on ivy and spring foliage has now become turgid enough to use without it wilting, and can be gathered from the garden or foraged from our hedgerows. Summer is here!

A Church Wedding in June

This delightful country church was the setting for a double celebration. Styling

Early profusion of summer flowers.

LEFT: Floral Church Arch

for the wedding was kept simple and playful with a country theme. The church was to celebrate its 800th anniversary a few days after the wedding, so the parishioners were ready with plans for their own flower festival. Mindful that we had to tie in with both the bride and the church flower-ladies, it was decided to decorate the inside of the church with the wedding theme and the outside church arch with a more elaborate design worthy of the forthcoming flower festival. Most of the floral arrangements inside the church were selected for a quick and clean removal, then taken and used again at the reception. The construction made for the rose arch over the door was, once used for the wedding, offered to the church for their own use. After the Sunday service following the wedding, each parishioner was invited to take a rose from the arch as a goodwill gesture from the bride. Recycling the flowers in this way made dismantling the frame much easier. As the arch over the door was facing west and away from the rays of the sun, the fresh, quality roses stayed in good condition for much of the following week.

The Church Arch

On their arrival via a long path to this old country church, guests were greeted by a compact arch of ivory and pink roses. Viewed from a distance, the arch seemed a solid colour, but on closer inspection you could see the delicate and feminine nature of the roses against a background of soft, variegated foliage. A frame of wood was superimposed with chicken wire, and floral-foam sausages were made and fitted to the church doorway. Variegated pittosporum covered the mechanics and the pink and ivory roses were added at random; pennycress was inserted between the roses at the top and foot each side of the

Pink and white roses to greet the bride.

arch to create further interest and some profile. Although the frame of the arch was based with foliage the day before the wedding, due to heavy thunderstorms that evening the roses were not added until 6am the following day.

Inside the Church

As the oak cover on the font is 400 years old, restrictions governed where and

Hessian sacks containing summer blooms.

how we could decorate it. Understandably no flower arrangements or water were allowed near the top of the ancient oak. Rustic hessian bags were placed around the font on the stone step at the base. The position of the font, in direct line with the chancel, gave the newly married couple a focus point on their retreat back up the aisle. The pretty pink colour blended in with the pink bridesmaids' dresses and the hessian texture was harmonious with the country theme. The bags were lined with plastic sheeting; and to keep the flowers as fresh as possible a square of wet floral foam was inserted flat at the bottom, which also gave the bags stability. This allowed the flowers to be arranged the day before the wedding and then placed into position on the morning. After the ceremony, the bags of flowers were easily scooped up by their handles and taken and reused on the tables at the reception venue. Gerberas, roses, sweet William, wheat, ivory freesias, and moon daisies filled the pretty country bags in a loose, open style fit for the setting.

The Aisle

As the aisle was very narrow, only just allowing two people to walk down it side by side without bumping into the floral decorations on the pew ends, it would only facilitate small arrangements of flowers on either side. Matching hessian bags were filled with peonies, roses, moon daisies, sweet William and stalks of wheat, which were tied to the wooden pew ends with clips and rustic string, bringing continuity to the rustic country theme. The flowers were arranged the day before and hung up just before the ceremony.

To blend in with the marble pillars of the church, beige urns placed on matching pedestal stands took two large, blousy arrangements of English country flowers, and were positioned either side

Small, rustic country-posy bags lined the aisle.

Light trails of ivy hanging from the rood screen.

of the chancel steps. The height was created with white delphiniums, and a soft outline was formed with garden fern and reinforced with larkspur, while stocks, roses and peonies made up the bulk of the design, and large hydrangea took up the focal area in the centre. A few natural wheat stalks were lengthened by taping them onto green garden sticks. These were popped in between the flowers at random to emphasize the country theme. The pedestals were arranged the day before the wedding and checked over and topped up with additional water on the morning itself. One pedestal was left for Sunday service, while the other was recycled and transported to the reception venue.

The Rood Screen

This very old rood screen was extremely fragile and had already seen some previous damage. Trails of ivy and small, loose hand-tied bunches of white peonies, spray roses, astrantia, and pennycress flowers were just enough to frame the entrance to the chancel without overloading the delicate wood. Soft, brown string was used to attach the small bunches of flowers to the wooden frame.

The Windowsills

Each of the four windows was dressed with two long trays of floral foam based with variegated pittosporum, soft pink and ivory roses, and sweet William. The profile of the arrangements was kept low to suit their main purpose as the top-table runner at the reception venue. The trays were made up and put in place the day before the wedding.

Roses filled the runners on the windowsills.

The Bride's Bouquet

This fun-loving bride's favourite flowers were gerberas and roses. Gerberas convey playful simplicity; add in English

country roses for her beautiful complexion, freesias for heavenly scent, a few garden sweet Williams and astrantia flowers for a natural look, plus wheat from the field for her rural upbringing. The bouquet was finished with a loose collar of traditional myrtle and although it was not in flower this gave off a very pleasant, aromatic perfume when touched. The handle was bound and tied off with a soft, rustic string. This neat and tidy, compact,

Bright, neat bride's bouquet with a country touch.

hand-tied bouquet reflected her orderly but joyful personality. The deep pink bridesmaids' dresses were used to select the colour for the flowers and acted as a foil against her ivory dress.

The Bridesmaids' Bouquets

Predominantly ivory flowers were chosen for the hand-tied bouquets for the bridesmaids, which contrasted against the deep pink material of their dresses. White peonies, white freesias, delicate pink spray roses, white sweet William, astrantia, natural wheat and ivory nigella were worked into a compact bouquet. The handle was bound and tied off with soft rustic string to match the bride's bouquet.

Bridesmaids' bouquets matching the bride's in opposite colours.

Bright, neat bride's bouquet with a country touch.

The Buttonholes and Corsages

Corsages for the wedding party were kept simple. There was a choice of ivory freesias and natural wheat, spray roses and freesias, and just spray roses, all

Fragrant freesia corsages.

with variegated ivy leaves. Making a variety of corsages enabled the guests to choose the option best suited to their outfit.

THE GROOM'S BUTTONHOLE
The groom chose to have an ivory rose with variegated ivy leaves, myrtle and stalks of wheat to match the bride's

Rose buttonholes for the groom's party.

bouquet. Simple, traditional ivory rose buttonholes were distributed to the best man, ushers and the bride's father.

Tip: If flowers are to be arranged and left outside overnight, check the weather report for adverse conditions.

The Reception Flowers

The flowers from the church were designed to be recycled at the reception. Windowsill runners were used to fit the top table, allowing the bride, groom and parents to enjoy the heavenly perfume of the roses at close quarters. Further runners were used on a side table along with the bridesmaids' bouquets. The hand-tied bouquets were put in vases to keep them fresh, allowing the bridesmaids to enjoy them for the whole day. The hessian sack posies from the font were placed in the centre of the guests' tables; one lucky guest from each table was chosen to take one home after the wedding.

Flowers and Foliage Used

Astrantia 'Pink Sensation'
Delphinium 'AJ White'
Delphinium 'Centurion White'
Dianthus 'Barb Mixed'
Dianthus 'Barb Pink'
Dianthus 'Barb White'
Eustoma 'Grand Arena Light Pink'
Freesia 'Du Volante White'
Gerbera 'Aqua Lollipop'
Hydrangea 'Verena Pale Pink'
Matthiola 'Lucinda Cream'
Nigella 'Damascena White'
Peony 'Duchesse White'
Peony 'Sarah Bernhardt'
Pittosporum tobira 'Variegatum'
Polystichum
Roses 'Grand King Arthur'
    'Baronesse'
    'Pink Piano'
    'Reflex'
    'White Avalanche'
    'Pink Avalanche'
Pennycress 'Green Bell'
Wheat

Chapter 10

Autumn

Autumn is a season full of rich colours, berries from English bushes and textures created by our deciduous trees and the fruits they produce. The season creates soft, mellowing leaves hanging onto their stems just long enough to enchant us with bright yellows, oranges, reds, pinks and copper browns. As this magical kaleidoscope of colour is transient, it is also difficult to capture at the precise moment we would like to use it, and we are left with bare, brown twigs in just a few short weeks. The fugacity of the colourful leaves therefore makes autumn foliage impossible to harvest from our countryside or gardens and what we do gather quickly becomes unusable if we want some plant material with leaves on. So because English foliage at this time of year can be tricky, and the theme easily lost, some other texture and contrast should be used to bring harmony to floral arrangements and help capture the season.

When styling autumnal arrangements it is much more effective to blend in with key areas, creating greater impact, and leaving other areas decorated to blend in with their natural background, adding further interest. Seasonal-looking plant material available from shops and wholesalers includes poplar, beech and eucalyptus, which are prepared with coloured dye and glycerine, altering some or part of their natural colour to shades of red, copper and bronze. Oak leaves are sometimes painted white or orange. Take care when handling foliage that uses these preserving methods, as it can leave the flower arranger with stained hands and clothes, something to be avoided when you will be in close proximity to bridal gowns. Seasonal English flowers are few in the autumn and may not be every bride's choice so nurseries from abroad have extended our supply by producing flowers including 'English' roses to bolster this limited selection. Other flowers including calla lilies are now available in beautifully harmonious tints and tones of yellow, orange, tangerine and burnt orange; also, coffee-coloured and even brown roses are available from imported stock from Holland, Columbia and elsewhere. It is now easier to match autumn colours with a larger range of flowers, which were previously regarded as being out of season.

Many types of berries are plentiful and available all year round but at this time of year you have a greater range in colour from white snowberries to cream, peach, orange and green hypericum. Also, blood-red and orange rose hips, common in our English hedgerows, are a valuable addition for texture and contrast. They create a rustic feel, and can be easily foraged provided you are prepared to de-thorn the very prickly stems, and leave some berries for our winter and migrating birds.

Castle Wedding in November

This romantic wedding was autumn-themed, incorporating the muted colours of period tapestries, seasoned oak, and drapes that depict topiary trees full of roses and fruits in pinks, reds, browns and gold. But as the bride wore an ivory princess gown with a full tulle skirt, colour inspiration was also taken from the bridesmaid's gold and autumnal bronze brocade dress. The romantic element was captured by using over 700 beautiful 'English' roses, some of which had the most intoxicating perfume. Further seasonal plant material was chosen to add contrast, texture and form.

LEFT: Castle entrance, peeping inside.

Main entrance viewed from above.

The Outer Castle Approach

The approach to the outer castle looked exciting and mysterious, leading guests to imagine what may lie behind the imposing gate. But as with many castles perched high into the landscape, it was subject to adverse weather conditions. Any tall standing floral arrangements on the outside of the castle walls would clearly not withstand such battering, so to welcome guests into this magical atmosphere and create some drama, low floral arrangements were created for either side of the gate. Long garlands of green ivy that blended in with the last reminiscence of greenery clinging to the ramparts were also made, along with a few climbing roses, defiantly outwitting nature with their last flourish of bright pink petals. Varieties of pink 'English' roses and green berries were added to make the entrance scene more inviting, and bring some warmth and enchantment back to this quaint castle. Two lions guarding the front gate were tamed with ivy garlands wrapped around their heads, which softened the approach and guided the guests into the courtyard. As ivy is quite hardy, lasting out of water for some time, the garlands were made the day before the wedding and laid out on the lawn overnight, while the roses and berries were added in the next morning.

The inner walls of the castle were usually ablaze with autumn leaves of Virginia creeper in pink, red and brown, but these had unseasonably disappeared all too quickly leaving the matching colours of the roses and foliage to stand on their own against a rather stark looking façade. Topiary trees lined the steps leading to the tall, studded-oak door of the main entrance. Ivy tops and ivy trails were used to construct the centre of the topiaries, multi-petal 'English' roses were added

Outer cobblestone approach.

Inner courtyard, main entrance.

for colour and perfume to complete the romantic look, and apples wired into the ivy introduced a Tudor touch to the trees. The treetops headed a crisscross rope stem mounted into sixteenth-century-style grey planters with the same crossing pattern, which also blended in with the grey stone steps. Long trays lined with floral foam above the top of the doorframe were filled with roses, hydrangea heads, bronze beech leaves and hypericum berries all to blend with the brown oak door. Matching roses, inserted into the bare Virginia vine on the walls either side of the door, cascaded down to connect to the topiary trees, making the entrance a continuous flowing movement from the top to the bottom of the steps. Although the theme for this wedding was autumn, topiary trees, which fit in with the period of the castle, would have traditionally been grown with evergreen plants. So the period style took precedence over the seasonal foliage. The trees were dressed with their greenery the day before and the roses and apples were added in early on the morning of the wedding.

Reception room, grand, white, marble fireplace.

The Reception Room

The warm reception room with soft, mellow oak panelling above the fireplace was brought to life with a full mantel display of flowers and foliage in matching autumnal colours. A run of cellophane was used to protect the top of the white marble before long plastic containers filled with floral foam were set down, ready to take the loosely arranged flowers. Brown and copper beech leaves, mellow yellow and pink roses, muted pinky-green hydrangea heads, hypericum berries and bare, brown twiglets of birch were added, keeping the arrangement low so as not to overwhelm and conceal the period panels. Varieties of light and dark pink roses also complemented the rich

colours in the carpet and the material on the settles either side of the fireplace. The hearth arrangement set in a large container filled with floral foam brimmed with matching roses, bronze chrysanthemum blooms, copper beech leaves and berries, taking the place of an open fire. The whole scene harmonized to capture the essence of the period, and the rich autumn theme. All the arrangements were worked on in situ the day before the wedding.

The Dining Room

The dark beams hanging relatively low from the vaulted ceiling of the snug

dining room were too imposing to be overlooked for dressing up for the occasion. A garland of green ivy, and pink roses and trailing red amaranthus softened the heavy, black oak and included the ceiling space into the whole scene. Two tall candelabras set on the table had no means of supporting the use of floral foam, so were decorated with hand-tied bunches of roses and hydrangea heads wrapped in tapestry ribbon and tied in place. To match the red velvet chair covers, a centrepiece of the deepest, richest red roses, apples and the red flower buds of *Skimmia japonica* were draped with passionflower vines, and arranged in a

Cosy castle dining room.

Rose posies on candelabras.

Aged oak beams swagged with garlands of ivy and roses.

Rich red rose and apple compote.

neat cushion design to complement the black lattice metal container. The cushion style was compact, leaving no space between each flower and piece of plant material. The neat style is somewhat reminiscent of the closely pruned shrubs seen in parterre gardens of the sixteenth century.

In contrast, the two further arrangements either end of the table

Free-flowing autumn arrangement.

The Bride's Bouquet

For the bride's unsophisticated but romantic hand-tied sheaf bouquet, a rustic seasonal look was created with colours chosen to complement the bridesmaid's dress and bring the whole scheme together. To make the bouquet a little more feminine, five pieces of soft, flowing, green asparagus fern were selected to trail down the bouquet, to establish the length and create movement. Seven, small, dainty, brown birch twigs were worked through the fern to add structure and texture to the design. Six stems of large orange rose hips were inserted to give colour and contrast. For the focal flowers, five roses were worked through the design with the support of three small dusky pink/green

hydrangea heads to elevate the bouquet at the tying point, which helped to give some profile. Further seasonal interest and texture was added with four long pheasant feathers wired and placed through the design. As some of the stems creating the tying point had become uncomfortable and quite twiggy, they were bound with matching tapestry ribbon to form a soft handle for the bride to hold. The light and wispy bouquet brought the season gently flowing down over the full tulle skirt of the princess dress. The bouquet was made on the morning of the wedding with the stems placed in water until a few hours before the ceremony.

A few wired and taped pheasant feathers, fern, rose hips and a matching rose were pinned into the side of the bride's loose hair to complete the picture.

The Groom's Buttonhole

A rose, feathers, fern, birch twigs and berries were wired and taped to make a buttonhole for the groom, all to complement the bride's bouquet.

were loose and open, matching the glorious autumn colours. Both table posies shone with golden brown, bronze and copper beech leaves, birch twigs, pink, peach and mellow yellow roses and blood red rose hips, untamed in a natural style and arranged in brown metal urns lined with green moss. A sprinkling of apples on a muted tapestry runner picked up the colour palette, finishing the luxury table design. The dramatic atmosphere was created with flickering candles, adding to the romantic look of the whole room, and as the room heated up the roses' hypnotic perfume began to fill our senses. The ivy garlands were made the day before the wedding and laid on the lawn overnight where the damp grass kept the foliage fresh. On the morning of the wedding the garlands were hung on the beams and the flowers were added at the last minute.

Bride's loose and open hand-tied shower bouquet.

Loose flowers pinned into the bride's hair.

Groom's autumnal mix buttonhole.

The Bridesmaid's Bouquet

As a contrast to the bride's bouquet, a simple hand-tied bunch of the deepest rich red roses, bronze chrysanthemums and shiny orange rose hips gave a luxurious autumn look for the bridesmaid. Wispy birch twigs and a few beech leaves tucked in added extra texture and interest. The bouquet was finished with a handle of soft hessian ribbon and gold cord to match the bridesmaid's dress. The bouquet was assembled the day before the wedding and the stems kept in water until shortly before the ceremony.

The Bridesmaid's Headdress

To create a light, rustic headdress, a circlet of beech leaves, birch twigs and two different sizes of rose hips were wired and taped onto a foundation of wires. The leaves, twigs and hips matched the colours and textures of the hand-tied bouquet, and only a few of the larger rose hips were used in order to keep the headdress light and comfortable to wear. The circlet was made the day before the wedding and kept wrapped in tissue paper until needed.

Bridesmaid's rich autumnal hand-tied posy.

Bridesmaid's autumn leaf and berry circlet.

The Best Man's, Fathers' and Mothers' Buttonholes

A varying selection of rustic buttonholes was presented to the main wedding party guests to choose from. Some buttonholes were wired and taped with brown stem wrap and some were just bound together with brown string. But they all blended in with the theme of beech leaves, twigs, rose hips and feathers. All the leaves were carefully wiped clean of any residue before assembling.

Mix of autumnal buttonholes for the wedding party.

Bride's bouquet at the feet of the lion.

Flowers and Plant Material Used

Amaranthus
Apples
  'Red Sentinel'
Beech leaves
Birch twigs
Chrysanthemum blooms
Hydrangea
Hypericum

'Magic Green'
Ivy
Long trails
Ivy tops
Partridge feathers
Skimmia
  'J Rubella'
Rose hips

Roses:
  'Ashley'
  'Baronesse'
  'Beatrice'
  'Edith'
  'Juliet'
  'Pink O'Hara'
  'Princess Charlene'
  'Wanted'

Chapter 11

Winter

Our winter gardens and countryside may look stark and dull grey, with trees stripped of their leaves left looking like bare skeletons of their former selves. You would be forgiven for thinking that all our flora was asleep and in hibernation. But on closer inspection, you can find under the layered blanket of leaves on the snow-covered woodland floor a few shy flowers that have popped their nodding heads up to show us their dainty white heads. Snowdrops are thought to have been brought to Britain by monks in the fifteenth century; the Latin name comes from the Greek *galanthus* meaning 'milkflower' and, *nivalis*, meaning 'snowy'. The hellebore (*Helleborus argutifolius*) comes into flower a week or so later; this is an evergreen plant that produces a cluster-head of lime-green flowers on long stems. These last several weeks, and are good for using whole in large arrangements, or as individual flowers picked off for wiring and gluing into buttonholes and headdresses. Garden varieties of hellebores and those bought from markets are available in many pretty colours, bloom sizes, and with double or single petals. The white

Helleborus niger is commonly called the Christmas rose. Colours vary from white and cream to pink and the darkest, almost black mauve.

Autumn flowers of *Fatsia japonica* have now wintered into creamy, white, plump berries on long stems protruding from the crown heads of the plant's branches, and are a welcome addition for adding texture and interest to bridal circlets and wirework. The flower heads of common ivy develop into plump black berries in the winter months and are equally useful for hand-tied designs, posies and wirework, but you would have to be quick to harvest these balls of berries before they are stripped bare by hungry, wintering birds. Another flower you may pick or forage from gardens, heaths and moors is white heather; garden centres also sell pots of heather at this time of year in various shades of white and pink. This dainty, light and long-lasting plant is very effective in all wire and glued wedding designs, bride's hand-tied and shower bouquets, and is particularly good for creating buttonholes with a Scottish heritage element. Available from the market, Persian buttercups are the roses of the *Ranunculus* family, with their full multi-

petal heads and striking colours varying from the most delicate pinks and creams to the strongest yellows, oranges and reds. Their heads are so heavy and full of petals that their soft stems curve gracefully under their weight. They are beautiful for hand-tied bouquets, but care is needed when inserting their soft stems into floral foam for table decorations.

Another flower that has been developed into large hybrids is the anemone, available all through our winter months, adding 'Jerusalem Blue' and 'Moron Red' to the winter colour palette. Their black centres coupled with black ivy berries can look very striking when used in jam jars for decorating tables or in a bride's hand-tied bouquet, but this soft-stemmed flower does not take well to wiring.

Many flowers can be bought from overseas, such as orchids, hyacinths and tulips. Tropical orchids come in many shapes, sizes and colours. They are long-lasting and very useful for all forms of bridal and wedding work. Cymbidiums (boat orchids), dendrobiums and phalaenopsis (moth orchids) can be wired or glued into the most intricate and delicate designs for shower

LEFT: White winter flowers at the base of a tall twig arrangement.

bouquets, crown headdresses, wrist corsages and necklaces, and can also be added to handbags and dresses. Hyacinths are grown in pots and are available as cut flowers from November to early spring – they are full of the most wonderful perfume and their little bell-shaped florets can be wired, threaded and glued. We think of tulips as spring flowers in the British Isles but they are imported and available from September to June, covering three seasons. Grape hyacinths are also available from November to May. They may well be thought of as a spring flower, but as their flowering season has lengthened so too has their use for bringing something blue into winter wedding designs.

Foliage such as the silver-grey *Senecio maritima*, with its lacy leaves, works well to interpret the frosty, wintery look in bouquets, and although available from the market it can also be grown in the garden and will survive moderately low temperatures. Also from the stark, dull, grey winter landscape outside, we can gather in and highlight twigs and branches with silver flourishes of paint and fairy dust to add a sparkling, frosted effect, or use some of the most vividly coloured flowers to add warmth and vibrancy to any winter wedding.

Silver circles around perfumed winter flowers.

A Winter Wedding

The seasonal flower choices and colours for this winter wedding were made not only to blend in with the bride's colours but as a complete contrast to the reds and dark winter evergreens used extensively in and around Christmas. Avoiding all the usual seasonal decorations gave this wedding a separate and original theme that was light, dainty and added a touch of sparkle.

A posy of winter flowers wrapped in silver twigs.

The Top Table

The top table at the reception was decorated with a line of posy arrangements made individually for reuse at, and for ease of transportation to, the evening venue. The posies, made in small, plastic dishes with floral foam, were encircled with twigs sprayed silver and wired into place, their centres filled with winter flowers in colours matching the overall theme. In the middle of the floral foam, little holes were made to assist the insertion of the fat stems of blue hyacinths, whose hypnotic perfume filled the room. White ranunculus, 'White Parrot' tulips, white lisianthus, light blue grape hyacinths and ivory orchids added an element of luxury, finishing off the central design. To keep the posies light, a small amount of blue sisal was added in between the flowers

A small spray of grape hyacinths and orchid on a napkin.

in place of any additional foliage. Small trails of variegated ivy were used around and over the silver twiggy base to soften the edge and add contrast. The posy rings were made up the day before the wedding and arranged on the table just before the wedding party arrived.

The Napkins

Crisp white napkins were dressed with a spray of blue grape hyacinths and ivory orchids tied with silver ribbon.

A bride's hand-tied bouquet with fleece detail.

The Tall Arrangement

A sparkly silver pot filled with floral foam was used to take tall silver twigs. Snowdrops, ranunculus and hellebores were added to the bottom of the pot to bring the whole scene together. The simple decoration was placed in the corner of the room where the winter sun shone onto the arrangement, highlighting the sparkly, icy effect.

The Bride's Bouquet

The bride's short, powder-blue dress was topped with a warm, winter ivory fur wrap. To match the fur, a collar of ivory fleece was made as a surround for a hand-tied bouquet before adding white lisianthus, white ranunculus, Christmas roses and white orchids for a touch of luxury, with snowdrops carefully inserted down in between the flowers to help support and separate their delicate

A groom's winter buttonhole.

A muff for a young bridesmaid to keep her hands warm.

stems. The fleece collar was decorated with ivory ribbon, which was used to bind in the stems of blue grape hyacinths chosen to complement the colour of the bride's dress. To dress the top of the bouquet a length of silver thread dotted with silver sequins was drizzled over the flowers and secured. The stems of the flowers were wrapped with matching fleece material and pinned in place with crystal-headed pins, creating a warm, soft handle. The collar for the bouquet was made in advance with the flowers added in on the morning of the wedding.

The Groom's Buttonhole

A Christmas rose, blue grape hyacinth and ivy leaves were wired and taped into a buttonhole for the groom. To make it individual and to match the theme the stems were decorated with silver wire crisscrossed down the stem and given a crystal-headed buttonhole pin.

A brooch for the bride's mother.

The Bridesmaid's Accessories

A muff was made of the same fleece material as for the bride's bouquet. The front of the muff was embellished with a decorative wire foundation in the shape of melting icicles; glitter dots were glued and placed down the ends of the icicles to add a sparkle. Blue grape hyacinths, snowdrops and Christmas roses were carefully pulled through the wire and

A brooch for the groom's mother.

glued into the framework. The muff was also lined with fleece to keep little hands warm and out of trouble. Flowers for this design had no water supply so were added to the muff a few hours before the wedding to keep them as fresh as possible.

Brooch-Style Buttonholes

These simple brooch-style buttonholes were made to match the floral decoration of the muff. The flowers were glued into place and a small magnet was glued to the back for attaching the buttonholes to outfits.

Flowers and Plant Material Used

Birch branches
Christmas roses
Grape hyacinths
Hellebores
Lisianthus
Cymbidium orchids
Ranunculus
Snowdrops
Tulips
Ivy
Sisal

Chapter 12

Spring

With its symbolism of new beginnings and rebirth, spring is the most traditional time of year to marry. The air has a feeling of freshness and anticipation. Spring bulbs have an astonishing rate of growth and bring a welcome flood of colour to the garden, cheering up the dullest of shady corners. Along with colour, the heady smell of perfume from 'bridal crown' and 'cheerfulness' narcissus begin to appear and contribute to the joys of spring. Hyacinths follow the narcissus, either grown on windowsills or in the garden, and are available now in yellow and peach along with blues, pinks and white. These heavily perfumed, petite bellflowers, picked from the main stem, last well when wired separately for including in headdresses, buttonholes, corsages and bouquets. Scented flowers are sometimes overlooked in favour of just a colour theme, but are a valuable addition to a wedding, adding an extra element for everyone to enjoy, when just a couple of bunches will fill any room with clouds of perfume.

Shrubs including Jew's mallow, forsythia and winter jasmine can now be used in place of winter greenery, which adds a light and bright airiness to arrangements of cut spring flowers.

Other garden flowers to consider include green *Helleborus foetidus*, otherwise known as the 'stinking' hellebore, and its cousin *Helleborus orientalis* (the Lenten rose), which come now in a variety of pinks and the darkest shades of mauve, following on from the white winter *Helleborus niger*. Grape hyacinths available in the winter from the flower market are now forcing their blue heads up past their foliage in our gardens. While they are a welcomed addition to our flowerbeds, their self-seeding habit can overwhelm small borders and they can become a nuisance in a few short years, so my advice is: pick them! Their little blue flowers are dainty and fresh-looking and can be wired in wedding work or will happily sit in floral foam for small posies.

In the flower market there is an ever-increasing variety of tulips in all sorts of colours and shapes, from sleek to multi-petal and even picot-edged varieties, making them a lovely choice for that extra-special spring bouquet. 'French' tulips have particularly large heads and very long stems, which make them useful for sheaf bouquets and large arrangements. The sleek, slender stems of tulips, if left to their own devices,

untreated with conditioning 'paper straightjackets', will twist and curve into interesting, graceful shapes as they strain to find the light (tropism), creating a more natural and sophisticated look. Ranunculus are now plentiful and can cheer us with bright oranges, yellows, fuchsia pink and reds, while the delicate colours of baby pinks, peach and china-white are ideal for matching to a classical-look bouquet. Although their stems are soft and damage quite easily, they last for weeks, increasing in size every few days before reaching fruition and looking their best with full and sometimes frilly tutu blooms – such a splendid spring flower for hand-tied designs. Anemones also have very soft stems and can be difficult to arrange in floral foam, but grow in the most vibrant of colours, including purple, red, lavender, bright and delicate pink, and white with a green or black centre.

From the countryside, we have sticky buds, the very tactile pussy willow and graceful, hanging hazel catkins blowing in the breeze. This robust foliage material conditions well and teams up nicely with garden or market-bought spring flowers. English bluebells are the most wonderful sight growing in woodland clearings devoid of any leafy

LEFT: Wooden mushrooms in a spring setting with a green sprite.

137

canopy to overshadow the effect of a
carpet of blue, the soft calming of their
faint perfume filling the air. But they are
best left undisturbed for future
generations to enjoy, as it is so easy to
buy 'English' or 'Spanish' bluebells from
the flower market, or create your own
supply by growing them in the garden.

A Spring Wedding

A bright and sunny spring day for a
wedding can capture the best of all
seasons as so many spring flowers come
with the advantages of bright colours
and perfumes. But their soft and hollow
stems could be a disadvantage unless
you use them in a sympathetic and
natural way. Little posies in jam jars,
where the stems can just sit in a little
water, are a sensible option. It is always
better to use flowers in the manner in
which they grow instead of forcing them
into styles and arrangements
unsympathetic to their nature. This is a
season of simplicity and spontaneity;
recycled jars with untamed natural plant
materials and flowers capture the true
spirit of the season.

In the example wedding, charming
little green sprites were hung in trees as
accessories to the scene; they danced in
and out of the branches in the breeze.
All the arrangements, jar posies and
twiggy structures were made the day
before the wedding, just leaving the
heart, the backs of chairs and the
bridesmaid's circlet to have their flowers
added in at the last moment on the day.
To get the bride's bouquet to look its
best, it was made fresh on the morning
of the wedding.

The young bridesmaid is carrying a
natural birch trug. The bluebells were
added to the trug to create the illusion of
the 'just picked' look. A few natural
dried mushrooms have been glued to the
top of the rustic trug for further interest.
In contrast, the handle was made easy to

Bride and bridesmaid under a tree.

Green sprite.

hold with a soft, pretty ribbon to match
the bridesmaid's dress. Her rustic circlet
is fashioned from natural, twisted vines,
blue and white wired hyacinth pips,
blue grape hyacinths and little rolled
pieces of birch bark, all to tie into the
theme and match the bride's bouquet.

The Bride's Bouquet

The bride held a bouquet of feminine,
curvy, trailing, twisted willow, carefully
defoliated of some of its large leaves,
along with bluebells and Eucharist lilies.

The bouquet was designed to
complement the style of the bride's
sleek, trailing dress. The flowers were set
in a floral foam bouquet holder to keep
them fresh, and the stems of the flowers
were used as a false handle coming out
of the other end of the bouquet holder to
create a 'just picked' look. A blousy blue
organza bow floated over the flowers,

Bride's bluebell bouquet.

covering the area where the stems and flowers joined. On the day, the perfume from the Eucharist lilies and the faint smell of the bluebells on the crisp spring air was heavenly. A few Eucharist lilies were wired and taped for inserting into one side of the bride's hair.

The Groom's Buttonhole

The groom's buttonhole had wired and taped grape hyacinths, a few small twiglets of birch, a green hellebore and a slither of birch bark added around the top of the stem. To give extra interest the wired stem was wound around a pencil to create a spring!

Groom's buttonhole: hellebore, grape hyacinth and twigs.

The Gate Decoration

This consisted of a natural twiggy heart, bound with spring blooms, white tulips, double blue grape hyacinths and just a few small pieces of green bell. Organza ribbon was tied to one side to create a soft movement in the spring breeze. The

Natural twig heart on gate with spring flowers.

heart was tied to the gate as an invitation for guests to step into the secret garden for the casual picnic reception.

Rustic Table Posies

A mix and match of recycled jam jars prettied up with sleeves of lace, string, wool and wood were filled with soft-stemmed spring flowers, grape hyacinths, bluebells, narcissus, anemones, birch twigs, ranunculus and

A selection of vintage jam jars on a rustic table setting.

Jam jars with spring flowers.

Spring Boxes

Wooden crates were used here for elevating, supporting and steadying a natural vegetative arrangement in a matching smaller box, consisting of pussy willow, guelder-rose, daffodils, anemones, bluebells, *Fatsia japonica* berries and hazel catkins. These spring flowers and foliage were chosen for their ability to blend in with the rustic surroundings.

Tree-hanging bottles sprouting spring flowers.

hazel catkins. The different heights and sizes of the containers added interest and contrast. The picnic tables were covered with a hessian and lace runner and slices of wood used for interest, texture, creating different heights and bringing all the elements together for a harmonious woodland scene.

Up in the bare branches of the trees, further interest was created with hanging bottles, again dressed up with lace and filled with bluebells, grape hyacinths, narcissus and hazel catkins. If you opt for an arrangement like this, make sure the bottles are tied securely and not over the heads of guests or at a height where they can be knocked into.

Rustic wooden crates used to elevate a natural vegetative arrangement of spring flowers.

The Picnic Basket

This willow picnic basket was used as a container. The flowers springing forth from its open lid are daffodils, pussy willow, guelder-rose, hazel catkins, white ranunculus and the berries of *Fatsia japonica*. These easily moveable containers were useful for carrying and placing around the picnic area.

Pretty Spring Blooms on Garden Chairs

The backs of the bride and groom's garden chairs were decorated with natural twiggy structures incorporating pink ranunculus, white tulips, bluebells and variegated ivy. All the securing paper wire was neatly finished, with any ends tucked into the back of the chairs amongst the flowers to avoid snagging.

Picnic basket bursting with spring flowers.

Garden chairs decorated for the bride and groom.

Close-up of flowers on garden chairs.

Chapter 13

Designer Wedding Brooches, Wristlets, Muffs and Bouquets

With the innovation of new products and materials, a variety of creative possibilities can be worked into bespoke bouquets, brooches and wristlets to a bride's specific design. This can set the bride apart from the norm and the work for the florist can be interesting, creative and challenging.

The best way to start any new design is to draw the shape in pencil first then apply the selected flowers. This way you can see instantly if the design will work and how it will look. There may be a lot of rubbing out and redrawing, but it is better to make a mistake in pencil than with fresh flowers. Plant material decisions may have to be revised along the way not only to create the look you wish to achieve but to accommodate suitable flowers. Not all flowers will bend, twist and live out of water for long.

Next you will have to decide on your construction method and what technical aids are required to successfully complete the design. The advantage for framework designs is that they can be finished and put aside weeks before a wedding. With all the design work done, you can easily add the fresh flowers shortly before delivering to the wedding

Simple wire brooch design.

party.

This chapter looks at using decorative wires and flexible canes in simple forms, allowing you to grow in confidence and expand your repertoire to include more experimental designs and challenging ideas as you progress.

Brooches

Bespoke Brooch

This brooch-style decoration is made from flattened bullion wire, which is an integral part of this simple design. As there are many colours of wire to choose from, various shades and tones can be selected to complement the wearer's colouring. Plant material is then glued

on and sequins are added to accessorize. The brooch is very lightweight and sits flat on clothing without dragging the material. A magnet is used to attach the brooch to a garment. Alternative brooches can be made on card and attached with a manufactured corsage pin, or a magnet. Whether this style is worn on a dress or lapel it can be made suitable for both men and women and decorated as elaborately or as simply as you wish. The following design is made as simple as possible for you to add your own creative ideas and accessories.

MATERIALS
2 sprigs of heather
2 small ivy leaves

Wire, glue and magnet.

LEFT: Wire frame with moth orchids, calla lilies and angel vine.

1 small hellebore flower
5 metres of bullion wire, plus 1 extra
metre for sewing
Cold glue
Sequins or beads

METHOD
Pull out the five-metre length of bullion
wire and jumble into a small pile.
  Play with the wire between your

fingers and manipulate it into the
desired shape. Try to even out all the
wire to fill any gaps, then flatten the wire
with the palm of your hand.
  With the extra metre of wire, sew the

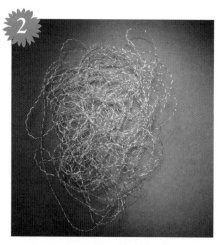

Jumbled wire.

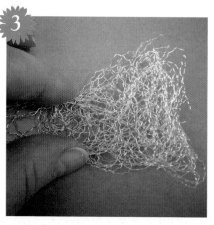

Manipulate the wire into your desired shape.

Sew together.

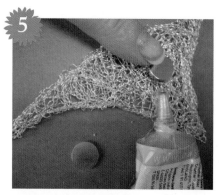

Glue one side of the magnet onto the wire.

Gluing plant material onto brooch.

Add ivy leaves and sequins.

Winter wedding
design with grape
hyacinths and ivy.

shape together by threading in and out,
paying attention to the edges. This will
help to strengthen the design. Tuck in
and secure any loose ends of wire.
Using the cold glue, apply a little on the
magnet and a little on the wire, wait
until tacky and press together.
  Trim all unwanted stalks that may
prevent plant material from laying flat.
Taking the sprigs of heather first, glue
onto the brooch one piece from the top

of the shape into the middle and one piece from the bottom of the design into the middle. Leave a gap in the centre and glue in the main flower.

Glue on the two ivy leaves and a few sequins.

Check no threads of glue are left behind, mist with water, place in a box and keep cool until needed.

Tip: To make it easier to part the two magnets, place a strip of paper in between them.

Wristlets

Wrist corsages, wristlets or bracelet floral designs can be made with flowers and/or plant materials and decorated with beads, ribbons and sequins. The flowers can be glued or wired onto a manufactured band or a hand-made construction that sits firmly and securely on the flat of the wrist. The designs should not protrude out too far so as not to interfere with any movement. Wristlets should be as light as possible and evenly balanced so the flowers do not fall to one side and are comfortable to wear. Any loose wires should be neatly secured and tucked in to avoid snagging. These designs can be made small and neat for the youngest of bridesmaids, or you might choose larger designs for older bridesmaids or statement pieces designs that may suit a bride. They are certainly a convenient option for leaving two hands free.

Wristlet

This wristlet fits an adult, but can be scaled down to any size by adjusting the length of the aluminium wire frame.

MATERIALS
2 ivy leaves
2 small orchid blooms
A few sprigs of viburnum flowers

Wrist design with orchids.

5 metres of bullion wire plus 1 extra metre for sewing
20″ (51cm) of aluminium wire
Cold glue
1 ribbon bow

METHOD
Make an oval bullion-wire foundation shape following all the instructions for the brooch at the beginning of the chapter.

Bend the aluminium wire into three lengths.

With round-nosed pliers twist the two ends of the aluminium wire into twirls, making sure that the ends are neatly tucked within the circles. Manipulate the wire frame by squeezing around the wrist to check the fitting. Any adjustments should be made at this point before adding the flowers.

Take the extra piece of bullion wire and sew the foundation shape onto the aluminium frame, covering the two twirls in the centre.

Ivy leaves, orchids, viburnum, glue and wires.

Bend the aluminium wire into shape.

Twist the ends into twirls.

Sew the foundation shape onto the frame.

Glue the ivy leaf.

Glue the second ivy leaf.

Glue the orchids in place.

Glue the viburnum into the design.

Glue the ribbon bow into the design.

Fitted onto wrist.

The finished wristlet design.

Glue the first ivy leaf into place with the stem end in the centre.

Glue the second ivy leaf in the opposite direction to the first leaf and wait until dry.

Glue the two orchid blooms on top of the ivy leaves.

Glue the small pieces of viburnum flowers in between the orchids.

Glue the ribbon bow onto one side of the design so the tails can drape over the wrist.

Wait until all the glue is dry before squeezing gently onto the wrist. The aluminium wire is so flexible that you can fit the wristlet into a comfortable position up the arm or low on the wrist. Taking it off and putting it back on will not damage the wire.

Mist with water and support with tissue paper, then lay in a corsage box. Keep in a cool place until needed.

Muffs

Muff Design for a Winter Wedding

As with the wristlet, bullion wire was used to make this icicle design for the bridesmaid's muff for the winter wedding in Chapter 11.

Bouquets

Wire-Frame Bouquet

Aluminium-frame bouquets can be worked into many interesting shapes and designs. The flexibility of the wire also allows you to make sculptured headpieces, handbags and baskets; you just need to add imagination!

MATERIALS
5 calla lilies
3 stems of orchid
A few pieces of angel vine
79" (2m) of aluminium wire
Ribbon, approximately 35" (90cm), to bind the handle and make a bow
Double-sided tape
Cold glue
Myrtle and/or bullion wire

METHOD
Pull out the aluminium wire and crumple it up into a bundle.

Locate and pull out the two ends of the wire at one-third of the overall length of the design.

Manipulate the aluminium wire into a teardrop-design shape. Make sure you leave the two located ends clear of the design.

With the palm of your hand, flatten the wire and adjust any large holes in the shape.

Pull the two wire ends out from the design and twist together to secure. Join in myrtle or bullion wire (your choice)

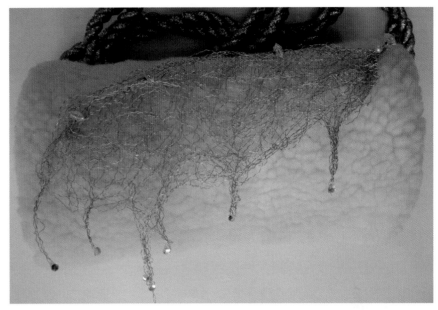

Foundation wire for muff.

Aluminium wire bouquet.

Ribbon, wires, tape, lilies, orchids and glue.

Pulling out aluminium wire.

Find the ends of the wire.

Shape the wire.

Flatten the wire.

Making the handle.

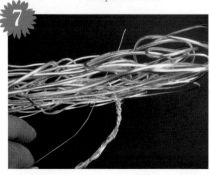

Secure the aluminium wire with myrtle wire.

Covering the handle.

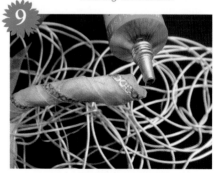

Glue to secure.

Adding calla lilies.

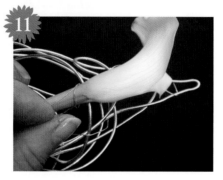

Secure lilies.

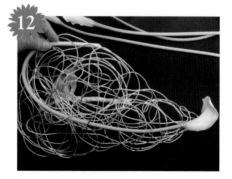

Secure lilies to top of bouquet.

Chapter 13 / Designer Wedding Brooches, Wristlets, Muffs and Bouquets

Add orchids.

The finished design.

Extended Heart-Shape Bouquet

An extension in shape, length or width can be created for a heart-shaped bouquet holder with the use of flexible canes to create a more interesting design. Canes are flexible and can form a structure on which to build and add alternative plant material and accessories. Advantages are that the bouquet is lightweight in proportion to

and secure the handle in place.

Thread the myrtle/bullion wire back into the main body of the shaped aluminium wire and sew in and out to secure and maintain the shape.

Using double-sided tape, cover the two wires that will form the handle and bind with ribbon. Finish by tying the bow close to the framework.

Secure the end of the ribbon with cold glue.

Weave the calla lilies through the aluminium frame from the bottom of the bouquet. As the wire is soft and flexible you can manipulate it to accommodate the stems as you go.

Secure lilies in place with myrtle or bullion wire. Tuck in the ends of the wire to avoid any snagging.

Weave lilies into and over the top of the frame and secure in place.

Add the stems of orchids in the open spaces to the other side to balance the design. Add the rest of the lilies to the top. Add the angel vine. Secure all the stems with wire.

The finished design is simple and stylish, using only a few beautiful blooms and leaving the silver wire showing through, as it is an integral part of the design. The wire can be made more decorative and prominent to create a different look, maybe for a Christmas theme or to match a heavily beaded dress. Additional interesting and textural plant materials can be draped over the design to enhance the look and add a personal touch.

An extended heart bouquet.

its size, and gives you a great foundation on which to use your creativity. Feathers and skeletonized leaves, sequins and beads or even lace could be used to co-ordinate with a bride's theme. The basic instructions for the following bouquet will, I hope, give you scope to embellish as you see fit, as your skills grow and your imagination unfurls.

MATERIALS
7 roses
5 bishop's weed heads
7 orchids
4 lily grasses
4 small lengths of willow
Thornless blackberry leaves to cover the base of the bouquet holder, plus a few for inside the design
12 midelino canes plus one other thicker cane
Cold glue
Diamante pins
Bullion wire
Lace ribbon to cover handle
Heart-shaped bouquet holder

METHOD
Cut the canes to a sharp point and insert into the frame of the bouquet, starting at the top.

Orchids, roses, bishop's weed, thornless blackberry leaves, canes, bullion wire, willow and cold glue.

Bouquet holder already prepared.

Add one slightly thicker, harder cane to the point of the heart at the bottom of the shape, and glue in place. This will stabilize the framework.

Bring down the first canes inserted to reach the bottom cane and secure with bullion wire. Allow some slack, needed to form the outline shape.

Add more canes in around the heart shape, weaving in and out of the first canes. Secure with bullion wire.

Mist the floral foam centre (do not saturate) with water, and add the roses, followed by the bishop's weed in small pieces to fill all the gaps.

Roll a few thornless blackberry leaves and stick them into the centre of the shape with diamante pins. Add the fine stems of willow on one side and secure with bullion wire. Add the lily grasses to the other side of the heart for contrast.

You can either wire or glue the orchid blooms in place.

An alternative design idea is to add more canes and lily grass down the centre.

Add more canes for a fuller-shaped design, and wire in place. Add two more roses with lily grass, but no willow.

Inserting canes into the frame.

Add central cane and secure.

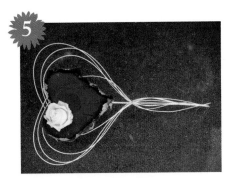

Adding more canes.

Inserting flowers.

Rolled leaves with pins.

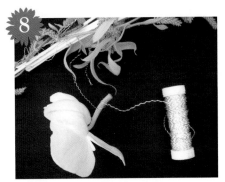

Orchids being added to design

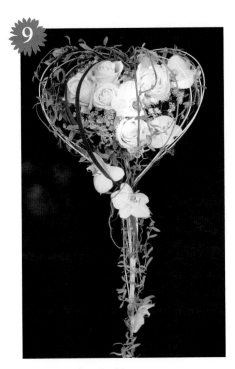

Finished bouquet.

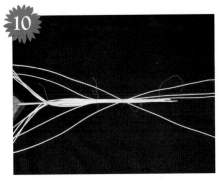

Alternative design.

Fuller design.

Plant Index

Latin name	Common Name	Latin name	Common Name
Alchemilla mollis	Lady's mantle	*Corylus avellana*	Hazel
Amaranthus caudatus	Love-lies-bleeding	*Cosmos atrosanguineus*	Chocolate cosmos
Ammi anthriscus sylvestris	Wild cow parsley	*Dahlia*	Dahlia
Ammi majus	Bishop's weed, Queen Anne's lace	*Danae racemosa*	Soft ruscus; Alexandrian laurel
Anemone coronaria	Windflower	*Delphinium consolida*	Larkspur
Anigozanthos flavidus	Kangaroo paw	*Dianthus barbatus*	Sweet William
Anthriscus sylvestris	Cow parsley	*Dianthus caryophyllus*	Carnation
Asparagus setaceus	Asparagus fern	*Dianthus plumarius*	Garden pink
Aspidistra elatior	Cast-iron plant	*Eryngium alpinum*	Sea holly
Aster ericoides	September flower, Michaelmas daisy	*Eucalyptus cinerea*	Silver-dollar tree
		Eucalyptus globulus	Eucalyptus nuts; Southern blue gum
Astilbe x arendsii	Florist spirea		
Astrantia major	Masterwort	*Eucharis grandiflora*	Amazon lily
Aucuba japonica	Spotted laurel	*Euonymus fortunei*	Winter creeper
Betula papyrifera	White birch bark	*Eustoma grandiflorum*	Japanese rose
Brachyglottis greyi	Senecio	*Fagus sylvatica*	Beech
Brassica napus	Rapeseed	*Foeniculum vulgare*	Fennel
Bromus lanceolatus	Brome-grass	*Freesia*	Freesia
Brunia albiflora	Silver brunia	*Galanthus nivalis*	Snowdrop
Calendula officinalis	Marigold	*Gerbera jamesonii*	Transvaal daisy
Calluna vulgaris	Heather	*Gleichenia polypodioides*	Coral fern
Caustis recurvata	Grandfather's whiskers, goanna claw	*Griselinia littoralis*	Variegated broadleaf
		Gypsophila paniculata	Baby's breath
Celosia argentea 'Plumosa'	Cockscomb, Chinese wool-flower	*Hedera helix*	Ivy
		Hedera helix 'Arborescens'	Ivy tops and berries
Centaurea cyanus	Blue Cornflower, bluebottle	*Helleborus foetidus*	Stinking hellebore
		Helleborus niger	Christmas rose
Centranthus ruber	Valerian	*Helleborus orientalis*	Lenten rose
Chondrus crispus	Irish moss	*Hyacinthoides hispanica*	Spanish bluebell
Chrysanthemum	Chrysanthemum	*Hyacinthoides non-scripta*	Bluebell
Cineraria maritima	Dusty miller	*Hyacinth orientalis*	Common hyacinth
Clematis (vines)	Clematis vines	*Hydrangea macrophylla*	Bigleaf hydrangea

Latin name	Common Name	Latin name	Common Name
Hydrangea paniculata	Panicle hydrangea	*Proteaceae*	Bridal crown
Hypericum androsaemum	St John's wort	*Ranunculus acris*	Common buttercup
Jasminum	Jasmine	*Ranunculus asiaticus*	Persian buttercup
Lavandula angustifolia	English lavender	*Rosa*	Rose
Lavandula stoechas	French lavender	*Rosmarinus officinalis*	Rosemary
Leucanthemum vulgare	Moon daisy or ox-eye daisy	*Rubus tricolor*	Thornless blackberry or Chinese bramble
Leycesteria formosa	Granny's curls	*Salix fragilis*	Pussy willow
Liliaceae	Lily	*Salix tortuosa*	Twisted willow, dragon's claw willow
Limonium	Sea lavender		
Lonicera	Honeysuckle, woodbine	*Scabiosa caucasica*	Caucasian pincushion flower
Lunaria annua	Honesty, money plant		
Lythrum salicaria	Loosestrife	*Scabiosa stellata*	Starflower pincushions
Malus	Apple	*Setaria*	None
Matthiola incana	Stock	*Skimmia japonica 'Rubella'*	Skimmia
Mentha	Mint	*Stachys byzantina*	Lamb's ears
Muehlenbeckia complexa	Angel vine	*Thlaspi*	Pennycress, green bell
Muscari armeniacum	Grape hyacinth	*Triteleia*	Triplet lily
Myrtus communis	Common myrtle	*Triticum*	Wheat
Nephrolepis exaltata	Sword fern, Boston fern	*Tulipa*	Tulip
Nigella damascena	Love-in-a-mist, Devil-in-the-bush	*Viburnum opulus 'Sterile'*	Snowball tree
		Wisteria	Wisteria
Paeonia lactiflora	Chinese peony	*Xeranthemum annuum*	Paper flower
Panicum virgatum	Fountain grass; swift grass	*Zantedeschia*	Arum and calla lilies
Papaver somniferum	Poppy seed heads	*Zinnia elegans*	Youth and old age
Phalaenopsis	Moth orchid		
Polygonatum grandiflorum	Jacob's ladder		
Polystichum munitum	Flat fern; Western sword fern		

Bibliography

Books

Blacker, Mary Rose, *Flora Domestica* (National Trust Enterprises Ltd, 2000)

Cooke, Dorothy, and McNicol, Pamela, *A History of Flower Arranging* (Heinemann Professional Publishing, 1989)

Emberton, Sybil C., *Shrub Gardening For Flower Arrangement* (Faber & Faber Ltd, 1965)

Gatrell, Anthony, *Dictionary of Floristry & Flower Arranging* (Hebe Press, 1998)

Gelein, Coen et al, *Decorative Cut Flowers* (Cassell, 1988)

Gilbert, Vanessa, Smith, Sarah, and Young, Lesley, *Foliage For Florists* (The Society of Floristry, 2006)

Hepper, F. Nigel, *Pharaoh's Flowers* (HMSO Publications, 1990)

Klett, Wally, *Wedding of Colour & Dreams,* (Herausgeber)

Lansdell, Avril, *Wedding Fashions 1860–1980,* Shire Publications Ltd., 1992

Owen, L., *The Professional Florists Manual* (British Florist Association and Society of Floristry Training Fund, 2014)

Pickles, Sheila, *The Complete Language of Flowers* (Pavilion Books Ltd, 1998)

Piercy, Harold, *Creative Ideas in Floristry & Flower Arranging* (Christopher Helm, 1989)

Putnam, Clare, *Flowers and Trees of Tudor England* (Hugh Evelyn Ltd, 1972)

Scott-James, Anne, Desmond, Ray, and Wood, Frances, *The British Museum Book of Flowers* (Imago Productions Ltd, 1989)

Smith, Willard S., Goldsmith, Margaret O., *Plants of the Bible* (Abingdon Press, 1989)

Spry, Constance, *How to Do the Flower* (Atlantis Publishing Co. Ltd, 1952)

Taylor, Jean, *Church Flowers Month by Month* (A. R. Mowbray & Co. Ltd, 1979)

Upward, Michael, *RHS Plant & Guides Perennials* (Covent Garden Books, 1999)

Acknowledgements

I need to thank a number of people who have both helped with, and made this book possible. Thanks to my daughter Claire for her unending support. Thanks to my son, Ashley, for his carpentry skills in creating the many props pictured here. To my granddaughter Holly, for such patience in being the perpetual bridesmaid, and my grandson Lewis for being the occasional stand-in photographer. Thanks to all of those, too many to mention, who contributed in so many different ways to the many, many photos used in this book. Also, thank you to my son-in-law for making copious cups of coffee and roast dinners, energy for the mind and soul. And finally, to my husband Paul for his patience, and putting up with my many 'moments' in creating this work and putting it together.

I would like to thank the following wedding venues for providing great backdrops for my flowers: Clevedon Hall, Clevedon; Walton Castle, Clevedon; Berwick Lodge, Bristol; All Saints Church, Clevedon; St Andrews, Congresbury.

I wouldn't have been able to complete this book without the fantastic photographs provided by the following professionals: Tim Rhys Davies, Jenny Hardy Wedding Photography, Tracey Robertson, Dr Rob Hawkins, Karl Barber, Aston Hue Photography. Claire Last from Blue Daisy Photography. Katherine Jo Bridal Designs and The Bridal Room for dresses.

My thanks to Meijer Roses for supplying the roses for the church arch and Alexander Farm Roses for the roses for the castle scene.

Index

Related Titles from Crowood

Commercial Floristry
Designs and Techniques
SANDRA ADCOCK

ISBN: 978 1 84797 377 1

Designing and Making
Hats and Headpieces

Judy Bentinck

ISBN: 978 1 84797 822 6

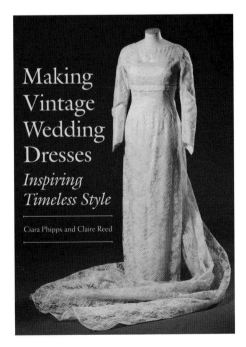

ISBN: 978 1 78500 312 7

ISBN: 978 0 85236 570 0